Word WISE & *Content* RICH

GRADES 7–12

*Word*WISE & *Content*RICH

FIVE ESSENTIAL STEPS TO TEACHING ACADEMIC VOCABULARY

Douglas Fisher and Nancy Frey

FOREWORD BY
KAREN BROMLEY

HEINEMANN
Portsmouth, NH

Heinemann
361 Hanover Street
Portsmouth, NH 03801–3912
www.heinemann.com

Offices and agents throughout the world

The authors and publisher wish to thank those who have generously given permission to reprint borrowed material:

Cover image from *The Great American Mousical* by Julie Andrews Edwards. Copyright © 2006 by Julie Andrews Edwards and Emma Walton Hamilton. Used by permission of HarperCollins Publishers.

Cover image from *George Washington, Spymaster: How the Americans Outspied the British and Won the Revolutionary War* by Thomas B. Allen. Copyright © 2007 by National Geographic Society. Reprinted with permission of National Geographic Society.

(*continued on page 173*)

Library of Congress Cataloging-in-Publication Data
Fisher, Douglas.
    Word wise and content rich, grades 7–12 : five essential steps to teaching academic vocabulary / Douglas Fisher and Nancy Frey.
        p. cm.
    Includes bibliographical references and index.
    ISBN-13: 978-0-325-01382-4
    ISBN-10: 0-325-01382-9
    1. Vocabulary—Study and teaching (Secondary).   2. Language arts—Correlation with content subjects.   I. Frey, Nancy.   II. Title.
LB1631.F568 2008
428.1071′2—dc22   2008005323

Editor: Wendy Murray
Production: Lynne Costa
Cover design: Shawn Girsberger
Cover illustrations: John Graham
Inside front and back covers: Ogden's Basic Word List
Typesetter: House of Equations, Inc.
Manufacturing: Steve Bernier

Printed in the United States of America on acid-free paper
12 11 10 09 08 VP 1 2 3 4 5

Contents

Foreword

Middle and secondary school teachers, staff developers, and curriculum coordinators: Sit up and take notice! Here is a book you have long awaited and definitely need to own. For many years, or so it seems, vocabulary teaching in the content areas has suffered from neglect and misunderstanding. In *Word Wise and Content Rich, Grades 7–12: Five Essential Steps to Teaching Academic Vocabulary*, Doug Fisher and Nancy Frey make up for lost time, bringing academic word learning and vocabulary instruction to the forefront of good teaching.

The authors not only give the special considerations of content area teachers their fair due but also consider the unique learning demands of adolescents. They challenge accepted vocabulary practices such as "assign, define, and test," explaining why these practices should be abandoned once and for all (they don't work). They fully lay out the high stakes of this game: Vocabulary matters. Vocabulary affects students' comprehension, fluency, writing, speaking, thinking, learning, and achievement as well as their confidence. If we don't get word instruction right, we clip the wings of our students on many levels.

In separate chapters for each topic, they discuss, show, and provide practical ideas for ways to develop vocabulary through teacher modeling, peer talk, individual activities, and collaboration to provide a schoolwide focus on word learning. Finally, we have a resource that gives us an engaging way to embed vocabulary instruction in an array of daily teaching and learning processes.

This book, based on theory, research, and the teaching experiences of the authors and practicing classroom teachers, shows you how to become intentional in your vocabulary instruction so you can help your students become independent word learners. Because content areas teachers focus on teaching their subjects, and many of them assume their students learned vocabulary strategies in earlier grades, these teachers often teach new words ineffectively or leave little time for teaching them. But the specialized, technical vocabulary middle and high school students need to know in order to learn and achieve in school requires effective and efficient vocabulary teaching. Fisher and Frey provide a much-needed set of criteria for selecting words that warrant teaching, and they give readers a sound framework for teaching these words effectively and efficiently.

This book is unique in several ways. First, with examples and vignettes from various classrooms and a reader-friendly style, Fisher and Frey show us, but do not tell us, how to improve content area vocabulary instruction. Their real-life classroom examples make clear how to use such things as context, morphology and word parts, peer interactions, reciprocal teaching, and graphic organizers to help students learn words in science, social studies, math, English, and other subjects. As well, they include an entire chapter on individual activities for teaching academic vocabulary. Many examples of student work, teaching materials, drawings, photographs, and charts support and enliven the text, showing how these ideas work in the real world of adolescents in middle and secondary classrooms.

A second unique feature of *Word Wise and Content Rich* is the authors' translation of theory and research into practice. While theory and research thoroughly ground the book, Fisher and Frey have seamlessly woven both into the fabric of the text in such a way that it is an enjoyable read. The authors' style persuades the reader that the strategies and ideas they present have a sound basis, and at the same time, they clearly describe and explain each strategy and activity. Additionally, in the last chapter the authors provide theory- and research-based professional resource materials for further reading about building students' academic vocabulary.

A third unique feature of this book is Fisher and Frey's notion of a school-wide focus on learning words. No other book on vocabulary teaching that I know of addresses this important aspect of word learning. If vocabulary teaching is to have an impact on all students, then everyone needs to share a common perspective on it, and this perspective and the accompanying practices should pervade the entire faculty and school. Fisher and Frey address this notion and offer practical ideas for raising the word consciousness of both teachers and students.

Word Wise and Content Rich is an important book for middle and high school teachers, staff developers, and curriculum coordinators to own. As I read my prepublication copy in order to write this foreword, it occurred to me that this book is a natural for a teachers' study group. It is well worth the time spent reading and discussing with colleagues because the ideas it holds are basic to rethinking and transforming vocabulary teaching. Fisher and Frey's recommendations about teaching academic vocabulary are not only important and timely but also critical to student learning in every subject area.

Karen Bromley
Distinguished Teaching Professor
School of Education
Binghamton University
State University of New York

Words (Still) Matter in Middle and High School

1

D'Andre sat in his U.S. history class, reading over a worksheet that featured ten vocabulary words, including *suffrage, amendment, appeal, ballot, constitution, hero,* and *register.* His task was to alphabetize the list, write definitions for each word, and then use each in a sentence. Like many of his classmates, D'Andre spent the next fifteen minutes diligently looking up the words in dictionaries and in the textbook's glossary before cobbling together the definitions. Adapting one of the meanings in the dictionary for the word *appeal,* D'Andre defined it as

> attractiveness that interests or pleases or stimulates

He then wrote a sentence containing the word *appeal*:

> Shawna appeal to me from her good looks.

D'Andre slogged through the rest of the task, completing definitions and sentences for the other nine words designed to introduce students to the unit of study. For some of the words, you could see D'Andre understood the topic at hand, while his work on other words displayed that he was not making worthwhile connections between this exercise and the historical context. It's not surprising, then, that the task did not get D'Andre any closer to mastering the content standards focused on women's suffrage. Nor did this vocabulary task prepare him for the reading he was expected to do next, the reports he was expected to write, or the classroom discussions he was expected to participate in.

The vocabulary work took class time but did not scaffold his understanding of content in any significant way. Classmates of his who did "better" (by getting closer to the word) than him on the task also lost precious class time, for the task didn't deepen their knowledge either.

Quite frankly, we don't have time to waste on ineffective approaches. Vocabulary development in secondary classrooms is critical, and yet few teachers feel surefooted about how to achieve it. It seems as though over that last few years there has been more attention in the field to the issue of teaching academic vocabulary—lots of declarations that if students are to learn in history, science, math, English, art, music, physical education, and the myriad of classes they complete in middle and high school, they must become familiar with content-specific vocabulary—yet when we looked to the research base for next steps, we found it's scant for secondary school. Most of what we could find was written from research and practice developed for elementary classrooms. Our motivation for developing this book was to discover what works in improving academic vocabulary for middle and high school students. What could be applied from the elementary research, and what didn't transfer well to older students? What works especially well with older students?

And so we set out to identify effective practices for secondary schools. We tried them out for ourselves, in our own classrooms as well as the classrooms of our friends and colleagues, to determine how students could be engaged with academic vocabulary learning. In addition, because we have tracked the implementation of these approaches using both quantitative and qualitative measures to ensure that they are effective (see, e.g., Fisher 2007; Fisher and Frey 2008), we feel comfortable making specific recommendations.

■ The Unmet Vocabulary Needs of Secondary Classrooms

The body of research on vocabulary knowledge is deep and broad, and as secondary educators, we are grateful for what is known about the volume, types, and range of words students typically acquire during their primary years. However, there has been relatively little work done on how this knowledge applies to the demands of middle and high school classrooms. In particular, academic vocabulary development at the secondary level is constrained by these facts and perceptions:

- The school day is subdivided into fixed periods of anywhere from fifty to ninety minutes, limiting the amount of time that can be devoted to vocabulary instruction.

- Secondary students are forced to shift cognitive and conceptual gears every fifty to ninety minutes and work with four to eight different teachers each day, who dedicate varying amounts of time to vocabulary instruction.

- Secondary schools operate within but rarely across content areas. Therefore, students and teachers operate within silos with limited cross-content vocabulary development. For the most part, teachers have little sense of what vocabulary students have learned in other courses.

- The sheer volume of content standards is daunting for teachers and students alike, resulting in a perception that there's no time for vocabulary development because it limits teachers' ability to cover the content.

- Vocabulary development is widely perceived as being the responsibility of the English department.

- Content area teachers know their vocabulary, but many know relatively little about effective instructional practices for vocabulary development. Hence, too many secondary students are taught (but do not necessarily learn) academic vocabulary in much the same way as D'Andre.

Student engaged in word sorting in Earth Science

■ Learning from Our Postsecondary Colleagues

As a middle school or high school teacher, you may even believe that you shouldn't have to work so hard to make up for all the vocabulary and reading comprehension teaching that *didn't* happen before your students sauntered through your classroom door. Guess what? *We have to get over it.* Lack of vocabulary knowledge holds serious ramifications for the secondary student, so there is no time for finger-pointing. And to look on the bright side, if we can become successful at developing our students' word knowledge, their reading comprehension and academic achievement will dramatically improve. Word knowledge is directly related to a learner's content learning, especially through reading (see Flood, Lapp, and Fisher 2003).

Research conducted with struggling college students offers us some clues about just how students' word knowledge relates to reading proficiency. This research, which we think is underreported in secondary educational research, has much to teach us; after all, struggling college students were recently sitting in high school classrooms. For instance, a study of 165 college freshmen enrolled in a remedial reading course found that vocabulary was the only variable that made a statistically significant contribution to measures of literal and critical reading comprehension, evaluation, and appreciation of reading materials (Farley and Elmore 1992). Baker examined the habits of lower- and higher-achieving college freshmen (as measured by the verbal portion of the SAT exam, which includes vocabulary) as they read informational text passages. She discovered that the less-able readers were "less likely to challenge passage truthfulness . . . and they also identified fewer word level problems" (1985, 308). These findings affirm what many secondary educators have long known: students with smaller vocabularies and lower comprehension levels read with more trepidation, question the text less, and fail to notice when they don't understand something. A study by McKeown (1985) showed a similar disparity in general reading skills between less-skilled students with small vocabularies and high-ability students. Specifically, the study pointed to differences in the reasoning processes used by high– and low–verbal ability students as they tried to figure out word meanings. The less-skilled students (1) had a *limited use of context*, in that they focused too narrowly on the context and failed to consider key aspects that were needed to derive the meaning of the target word; (2) *attributed the meaning of the entire context to the target word*; and (3) *went beyond the limits of the meaning of the context* to develop a scenario into which a meaning might fit.

Another study of interest to us focused on the vocabulary knowledge of college freshmen reading above and below grade level (Francis and Simpson 2003). The researchers were interested in discovering students' beliefs about how vocabulary is studied and learned. Much to the surprise of the researchers, both study groups were unprepared to learn vocabulary on their own, believing instead that the only way it could be learned was through rote memorization of lists. Further, the students in the study did not see why it was necessary to recall vocabulary beyond a weekly test, and both groups scored poorly on using vocabulary meaningfully in writing. The authors pointed out that students' beliefs and perceptions left them ill equipped to self-regulate their learning, a vital skill in college.

With this book, our goal is to show you a teaching and learning framework that helps students become self-regulating, independent word learners. We want to move the profession's thinking hundreds of miles away from the view of vocabulary instruction as disembodied lists for students to memorize and toward a stance where word learning in the content areas is fun for students, is an excuse to interact with peers, and gives them the intellectual and social currency of being able to think, speak, read, and write with greater facility.

An Intentional Vocabulary Model

We've organized the rest of this chapter around the topics that middle and high school teachers often bring up when discussing vocabulary learning. We consider what research and our own teaching experiences have to offer on these issues, so that we all have a common ground on which to build. Each of the following chapters focuses on one facet of vocabulary development in middle or high school classrooms. Taken together, these facets provide you with an *intentional vocabulary model* that can transform students of all abilities into proficient readers, because they bring to texts banks of word knowledge that help them access the language of ideas. Students become proficient writers, too, for their vocabularies help them say what they mean—and convey what they know.

Why Spending Time on Vocabulary Is Worth It

Vocabulary is among the greatest predictors of reading comprehension (Baker, Simmons, and Kameenui 1998), and reading comprehension, it almost goes without saying, is central to learning in the content areas. The relationship between vocabulary and reading proficiency is so powerful that there is evidence that vocabulary size in kindergarten is an effective predictor of reading comprehension and academic achievement in the later school years (Scarborough 2001).

If you doubt this, consider the fact that missing just 5 percent of the words in a text makes it nearly incomprehensible. Five percent doesn't sound like a lot, but try to read the text in Figure 1.1, from which we have removed 5 percent of the words and replaced them with nonsense words. You may glean that the text is about coffee, but you'd have a hard time answering questions about the meaning, right? In this case, you probably have significant background knowledge that you can use to fill in the gaps in your word knowledge. Imagine if you had limited background knowledge about the topic and didn't know the words. The text would be incomprehensible.

Now consider the role that vocabulary plays in writing proficiency. We know that writing is thinking. (Have you ever tried to write and not think? Impossible.) So, how does a writer think? He thinks in language, in words. In general, the more words a person knows, the better he is at writing. And the better he is at writing, the better he is at thinking. We know that this sounds like circular logic, but it reflects the recursive nature of reading and writing. As students learn, they acquire labels for ideas. As they think, they can use those labels. As they write, they clarify their understanding of those ideas and even generate new understandings. Writing is evidence of the incorporation of information. Extensive vocabularies help one refine one's thinking through more nuance and sophistication. Word knowledge, in a sense, makes us smarter.

Factoid 1

Caffeine is tasteless. A "strong" wepuha is mostly the result of the amount of coffee in relation to the amount of water. The longer a bean is sisku, the less caffeine it has. "Arabica" beans have less caffeine than "Robusta" beans. "Arabica" beans have more flavor than "Robusta" beans, which are mostly used in high-volume coffees and instant coffees.

Factoid 2

Wepuha is the way the bean is edusca, not the bean itself. You can use many different balksiks to produce wepuha coffee. You can also use the wepuha roasted coffee to make a larger cup of coffee. In the United States, wepuha roasting results mostly in a darker roast than wepuha roasting in Europe.

Figure 1.1 *Checking comprehension when 5 percent of the words are unknown*

Suffice it to say that vocabulary instruction improves writing (Fisher, Frey, and Williams 2002; Stevens 2006).

Knowing a Word: Deep Connections and Passing Acquaintances

What does it mean to know a word? Is it to recognize it? To be able to define it? To use it correctly—in all of its shades of meaning—in our verbal and written language? Consider the word *provocative*. You've heard it and no doubt used it. But think about the depth of word knowledge required to use this word well. As a case in point, an editor wrote in the margin of our book draft, "This is quite provocative!" We knew she meant challenging, thought provoking, not that our statement about reading aloud was the stuff of a romance novel. But would a seventh grader be able to tease out the appropriate meaning from context? Wise word users have a depth of knowledge that allows them to do so.

Beck and her colleagues (2002) get at this idea by distinguishing between shallow and deep word knowledge. By shallow word knowledge, they mean that students memorize definitions and do not have the deeper knowledge of the concepts that the words represent. To extend their metaphor, the range of people's word knowledge is like the difference between the shallow end of a swimming pool, the deep end, and the deep blue sea (in the case of linguists who know several languages or those well versed in word histories). While our middle and high school students might not reach deep-sea levels of professional linguists, our goal as content area teachers ought to be that they are able to know words deeply enough that they can use them flexibly across their content area courses, something we look at in more detail in later chapters.

So, depth matters. That is, knowing the multiple meanings of words matters, and reasoning a word's meaning in context matters. This view of vocabulary is relatively new. Vocabulary knowledge studies from the 1940s and 1950s focused on recall and recognition, usually through one-trial learning, followed by a quiz asking participants to list words when given the meaning (recall) or to identify the correct word on a multiple-choice test (recognition). Researchers soon saw the limitations of this kind of contrived measurement, especially because it did not reflect the ways in which vocabulary knowledge is authentically used. (But you can see how this recall-and-recognition approach continues to dig its claws into instructional ideas.) Measurement of vocabulary knowledge has since been refined to assess five dimensions:

- *generalization* through definitional knowledge

- *application* through correct usage

- *breadth* through recall of words

- *precision* through understanding of examples and nonexamples

- *availability* through use of vocabulary in discussion (Cronbach 1942, cited in Graves 1986)

Dale, O'Rourke, and Bamman (1971) further refined our concept of vocabulary knowledge by noting that words do not simply fall into two categories, known and unknown. Instead, there are degrees of knowing a word. Their continuum consists of four stages:

1. having never seen or heard the word;

2. having heard the word, but not knowing what it means;

3. recognizing the word in context; and

4. knowing and using the word.

The problem with the vocabulary worksheet D'Andre and his classmates were given was that it didn't really measure the depth of students' word knowledge across these four phases. D'Andre had shallow word knowledge, and the poorly designed worksheet task allowed him to go down the wrong path—working with the wrong word meaning—without realizing it. If D'Andre had gone into the task with a deep knowledge of the word *appeal*, he might have written something like "I appeal Shawna's rebuff of my appeal." A stronger vocabulary activity would have scaffolded students' understanding more, guiding D'Andre to consider context when choosing between the meaning of *appeal* as attraction and *appeal* as in to take a case to a higher court.

Helping Adolescents Know What They Need to Know About Words

Here is where we step beyond the elementary vocabulary literature to consider the unique learning demands on adolescents. At some point, students must move from merely learning words to learning *about* their own learning of words. The role of metacognitive awareness in the learning lives of middle and high school students is critical in their continued development as self-regulated learners. The National Research Council (1999) has had quite a bit to say about this. It defines *metacognition* as "people's ability to predict their performances on various tasks . . . and to monitor their current levels of mastery and understanding" (12). Learning, after all, isn't just about being able to recall infor-

Students using phones to send text messages

mation; it is a process enacted upon by the learner. When you hear talk about "active learning," you're hearing the rumble of metacognition. A goal of teaching for metacognitive awareness is that students develop an adaptive expertise so that they can apply what they know flexibly and use it to learn new skills—analogous to the difference between being able to follow a recipe and creating a new one (Hatano and Ignaki 1986). This speaks directly to the findings regarding those college freshmen, even those who read above grade level, who did not possess an understanding of how or why vocabulary learning was necessary, nor did they know how to go about learning vocabulary beyond rote memorization (Francis and Simpson 2003).

Now think about this: When was the last time you acquired new vocabulary by writing a list and then memorizing it? Let's say you bought a new hybrid phone and dove into the instruction manual so you could operate it. Undoubtedly you encountered words you knew (*phone*, *camera*, *address book*), words you partially knew (*multiconnector*, *messaging button*), and terms that were completely foreign to you (*SIM card*, *Bluetooth*). First, you noticed what you knew and didn't know (monitoring). Then you set about learning the terms you didn't know because you recognized that you couldn't understand the manual without knowing these words. You looked at the diagrams and compared them with your phone. You checked the back of the manual for a glossary. You may have even enlisted the help of a tech-savvy teenager to give you a hand. The point is, you could predict the likelihood of your success with the task, you knew you needed to master the vocabulary, and you knew how to help yourself learn it. That's metacognition at work.

Similarly, secondary students need to be taught how to think metacognitively as they acquire vocabulary knowledge. Teachers should model their own thinking as they encounter words in text that might be confusing and show students how they figure out those terms. As we will also see, students need rich oral language experiences that cause them to utilize new vocabulary in discussion and clarify and refine their understanding of words with peers. They also need to learn strategies for helping themselves when reading independently, especially in getting unstuck when they encounter a tricky term. Ultimately, academic vocabulary development is as much about problem solving as it is about acquisition.

The Vocabulary Numbers Game

One of the most common questions middle and high school teachers ask concerns the number of words that students need to know to be successful. Nagy and Anderson (1984) noted that students would come in contact with 88,500 word families by the time they complete high school. Word families are groups of words consisting of the same root or base and their associated compounds and derivates. The poet Francisco Gomes de Matos used his knowledge of word families to create a poem about reading, which can be found in Figure 1.2.

These 88,500 word families translate to about 500,000 individual words. Thankfully for readers and their teachers, about half of these word families are used so rarely that students will likely encounter them only once in a lifetime. (For example, it's unlikely that you will ever need to know that *blepharospasm* is an involuntary twitching of an eyelid, unless you are an ophthalmologist.)

```
READING is forming
           informing
           reforming
           transforming

READING is ascending
           descending
           transcending

READING is lightening
           delighting
           enlightening

READING is covering
           recovering
           discovering

READING is conceiving
           receiving
           perceiving

READING is mind-using
           mind-musing
           mind-amusing
           mind-infusing
```

Poem by De Matos, F. G. (2007, Jun/Jul). Reading is . . . *Reading Today*, 24 (6), p. 19. Reprinted with permission of Francisco Gomes de Matos and the International Reading Association.

Figure 1.2 *"Reading Is . . . ," by Francisco Gomes de Matos*

But even reducing the number of word families and words a student needs to understand by half is overwhelming, especially if you think that you have to directly teach all of these words! If a student needs to know 250,000 words and has 180 days of school a year for thirteen years, that student will have to learn 107 words per day and never be absent. As we will see throughout this book, students learn a lot of these words while reading. Other words must be explicitly, systematically, and intentionally taught. They key to improving student achievement is knowing the difference between words students will learn automatically and which need to be taught.

Differences in the Types of Words Students Must Know

Over the past decade, a great deal of agreement has been reached about vocabulary instruction. In general, experts agree that there are three types of words that

General (Tier 1) Words	Specialized (Tier 2) Words	Technical (Tier 3) Words
hero	appeal	suffrage
gender	constitution	amendment
widow	register	ballot
married	pioneers	electoral
unmarried		Nineteenth Amendment to the United States Constitution
eligibility		feminism
advocate		
universal		

Figure 1.3 *Vocabulary words for women's suffrage unit separated by category*

students need to know. Beck, McKeown, and Kucan (2002) identify these as Tier 1, Tier 2, and Tier 3 words. In the world of secondary schooling, Vacca and Vacca (2007) identify these words as general, specialized, technical. If D'Andre's teacher had used this classification system, the words she selected might appear in the categories identified in Figure 1.3. We use these classifications to carefully select words for systematic instruction (see Chapter 2).

GENERAL VOCABULARY

By Tier 1 or general vocabulary, these researchers mean words that are basic for reading. These words are typically in the spoken vocabulary of most students and rarely need to be taught. Unfortunately, in many secondary school classrooms, instructional time is wasted on explicit instruction for words students could learn in other ways. These words are acquired as students read and are read to (see Chapter 6 for more information about this). General vocabulary words are not conceptually difficult, either, and are especially appropriate for learning through wide reading.

SPECIALIZED VOCABULARY

Tier 2 or specialized words are those high-utility terms that often change meaning in different contexts. They are words that confuse most readers and are significantly undertaught in most middle and high school classrooms. This category also includes words for which students know some part of the meaning, but do not have mastery of the complexity of the words' meaning. These words are critical for understanding. Imagine the student who is working with the word *expression* as it relates to a character's expression in a novel for English. The very next period, the student might be expected to write an expression in her math class. D'Andre's teacher acknowledged that this category of words was critical for understanding the text the students were to read but failed to recognize the effect that multiple meanings and context have on words such as *appeal, constitution, register,* and *pioneers.*

As another example of the power of these specialized words, read the following sentence from a sixth-grade textbook:

> Catherine the Great, a minor aristocrat from Germany, became Empress of Russia when her husband Peter, the grandson of Peter the Great, was killed.

The specialized word in this sentence is *minor*. To test our hypothesis that students use context in determining word meaning, we asked one hundred fourth graders, one hundred seventh graders, and one hundred tenth graders what *minor* meant in this sentence. On a multiple-choice test, the majority of fourth graders indicated that Catherine the Great was "digging for gold" when she met her husband. Interestingly, the majority of seventh graders got the question right, selecting the response that she "wasn't very important." The highest percentage of incorrect answers came from the tenth graders (70 percent), who selected the choice that Catherine the Great was "underage when she married Peter."

Again, context matters. Students use what they know and are familiar with to determine word meanings. In California, fourth graders study the Gold Rush and in tenth grade students think about their age all of the time as they wait to drive, vote, and legally enter a bar. To ensure their understanding of this text, the teacher would have to attend to the word *minor* by providing students multiple opportunities to use this specialized term in different contexts. This might occur through word sorts, word maps, or writing tasks.

TECHNICAL VOCABULARY

Tier 3 or technical words are those that are bound to a specific discipline. These are the seductive content words that teachers love to focus upon: *concerto, mitosis, metaphor,* and so on. Sometimes these words need to be directly taught and other times they simply need to be defined. The decision to teach the word versus explain the word should be based on the future utility of the word and its relative importance in facilitating or blocking understanding. Again, conceptual difficulty plays a role in what gets taught and how. The term *mitosis* represents an intricate knowledge set in biology and defies simple definitional instruction, especially because of its contrastive concept, *meiosis*. (You may recall from your own biology classes that both are processes of cell reproduction, one asexual and the other sexual.) By contrast, it is possible to teach *concerto* through definition: it is an orchestral work featuring a solo instrument, often a violin or piano. There are deeper layers to *concerto*—Romantic and Baroque concertos, the *concerto grosso* and *concerto de camera*—however, goals of recall, recognition, application, and precision influence the amount of time an orchestra teacher will spend on instruction compared with the English teacher whose students are reading the novel *Bel Canto* (Patchett 2005). Most obviously, the important words to teach are those that are critical for understanding the text or the content.

For example, while reading aloud *The Great American Mousical* (Edwards and Hamilton 2006), drama teacher Deb Glaser chose to explain the word *metropolis*

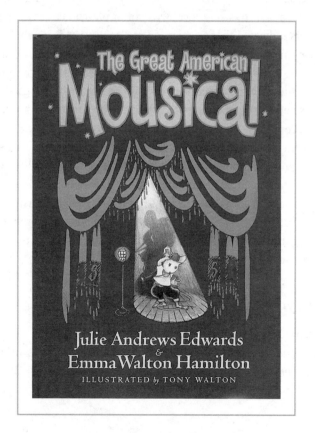

and not spend extended time on teaching it. The passage that opens the book reads:

> If you could stand upon a faraway star and look down on planet Earth on a cloudless evening, you might just notice a glowing pool of light . . . and chances are, that glow would be New York City. If you could leap from your star and fly down, down, down into the heart of that great metropolis, you would land in the most twinkling, sparkling place of all—Times Square. (1)

Ms. Glaser was more interested in the story that Julie Andrews and her daughter had to tell and knew that she would teach the words from the book that related to her content area, such as *scenery, balcony, orchestra pit, boxed sections, proscenium*, and *apron of the stage*. These words were consistent with the standards she wanted to teach and were words that students of drama should know. That is, they are the technical words that define her discipline.

■ Integrating Comprehensive Vocabulary Instruction in the Content Area

Sadly, vocabulary instruction in middle and high school classrooms is often neglected or occurs in ineffective, or even harmful, ways. To change this and increase the quality of vocabulary instruction requires a sustained focus on academic vocabulary. Secondary school teachers have to teach students *how* to learn new words, not just the meanings of specific words. If word learning occurred only through direct instruction, as some researchers suggest, then teachers would have to spend every minute of every day getting students to learn their daily 107 words. In contrast, we think that students should be taught how to learn words through a combination of wide reading, teacher modeling, *and* explicit, systematic, and intentional instruction.

We have developed an academic vocabulary model that consists of five big ideas. Each of the five big ideas is further developed in the chapters that follow. Taken together, this approach serves to develop the general, specialized, and technical vocabulary necessary for secondary student success, both inside and outside of school. For now, let's briefly explore each of the big ideas.

1. *Make It Intentional.* First and foremost, we have to intentionally select words that are worth teaching. We need to carefully consider the types of words students need to know and learn. Middle and high school students need to understand technical words to become proficient with the discourse of a discipline. They also need to know the specialized words that are commonly used but that change their meaning based on the context or content area in which they are used. The key here is to determine which words students need to know and how to best teach them. Accordingly, in this chapter, we focus on an instructional design model that is deliberate and takes into account what is known about human learning. Our intentional vocabulary learning model is based on a theory of gradual release of responsibility of learning, which suggests that teachers should purposefully plan to increase student responsibility for learning.

2. *Make It Transparent.* One way that students learn is through teacher modeling. The purpose of this component of academic vocabulary instruction is twofold. First, modeling develops what Michael Graves (2006) calls "word consciousness" by drawing attention to the language used by the writer. Second, it teaches procedures for problem solving unknown or poorly understood words. It is also important to discriminate between these two purposes and teaching specific vocabulary words. It seems reasonable to suggest that modeling word-solving strategies and word-learning strategies across content areas will help students learn words by providing them with cognitive guidance and a how-to model. However, using teacher modeling to teach individual words out of context is an inefficient use of instructional time. When teachers read aloud to their students and share their thinking about the words in the text, they develop their students' metacognitive skills.

3. *Make It Useable.* While we know that modeling is critical for student success, we also understand that immediately after this modeling, students have to use the words they've been taught if they are to own them. Students simply will not incorporate academic vocabulary into their speaking and writing unless they are provided multiple opportunities to do so. Collaborative tasks that require students to use newly acquired vocabulary verbally or in writing are thus a part of our model. Authentic usage is essential for acquisition of vocabulary knowledge.

4. *Make It Personal.* Independent learning is a vital but often undervalued aspect of word acquisition. In this strand of our model, students are given tasks that allow them to apply what they have learned in novel situations. This component is essential if students are to move beyond passive participation and incorporate new academic vocabulary into their funds of knowledge. Students have an opportunity to take ownership of the vocabulary by integrating it into their personal verbal and written repertoires.

5. *Make It a Priority.* We know that reading has an impact on vocabulary. Therefore, students must be engaged in authentic reading tasks, with texts they can read, on a daily basis. The best way to do this is to ensure that the school places a high priority on wide reading. In reading widely, students will acquire some of the general words they need to know. In addition, they'll see familiar words in diverse contexts and add new meanings to known words. In addition to wide reading, another schoolwide effort as part of our academic vocabulary initiative encourages all teachers to focus on high-frequency prefixes, suffixes, and root words. In doing so, they'll help students develop transportable skills they can use to make educated guesses about words they do not know. As we discuss later in the book, there are clusters of words that share meanings, and studying them together helps students remember them.

What Could D'Andre Do Had This Been His Experience?

Remember D'Andre's vocabulary task? Let's reengineer his learning through the lens of systematic, explicit, and intentional academic vocabulary learning. First, he would have read about the suffragette movement in class and at home. Doing so would have built his background knowledge and vocabulary. A list of sample books with a range of difficulty levels can be found in Figure 1.4.

At the same time, his teacher would have read aloud to the class and explained her thinking as she did so. She would have solved unknown words during her readings and modeled for students how they might figure out an unknown word. For example, had she read *A Time for Courage: The Suffragette*

Bausum, A. 2004. *With Courage and Cloth: Winning the Fight for a Woman's Right to Vote.* Washington, DC: National Geographic.

Fritz, J. 1999. *You Want Women to Vote, Lizzie Stanton?* New York: Putnam.

Monroe, J. 1998. *The Nineteenth Amendment: Women's Right to Vote.* Berkeley Heights, NJ: Enslow.

Rossi, A. 2005. *Created Equal: Women Campaign for the Right to Vote 1840–1920.* Washington, DC: National Geographic.

White, L. A., and N. Carpenter. 2005. *I Could Do That! Esther Morris Gets Women the Vote.* New York: Farrar, Straus and Giroux.

Figure 1.4 *Diverse books about women's suffrage*

Diary of Kathleen Bowen, Washington, DC, 1917 (Lasky 2002), she could have explained her understanding of *pickets* when she read "news of the pickets is spreading." She would have described her connection between a picket fence, with its sharp-ended posts, and the political form of picketing done by protesters carrying signs. She might even relate both of these definitions to the French military word *picquet*, which describes soldiers standing guard.

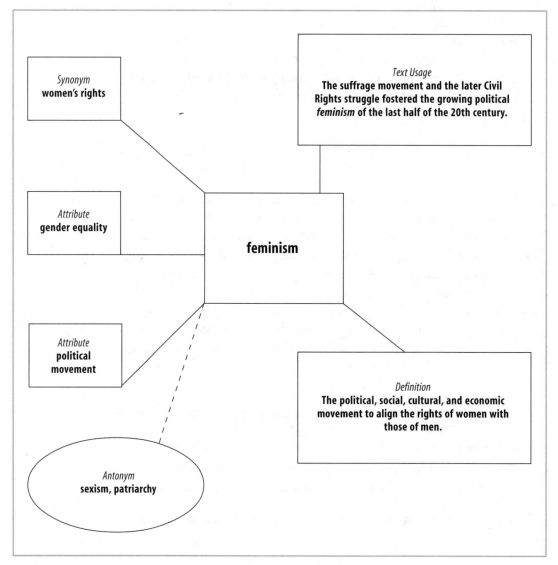

Figure 1.5 *Word map for* feminism

In addition, D'Andre's teacher would have focused instruction on the specialized and technical words she had selected. As is further explored in Chapters 4 and 5, she might have used semantic feature analysis, concept maps, text impressions, or vocabulary cards. For instance, she could have created a word map along with the class on the word *feminism*, like the one in Figure 1.5.

And finally, if he had been lucky, D'Andre would have been exposed to a number of prefixes, suffixes, and roots that related to the words under investigation. His teacher could have shown her students that *amendment* contains the root word *amend*, meaning to change or alter something, usually for the better. The addition of *-ment* changes the verb to a noun, and further refines the meaning, since this suffix is used to describe a process or action.

This intentional, comprehensive approach to vocabulary development would have strengthened D'Andre's vocabulary knowledge inside and out of this content area. In addition, he would have developed a deeper conceptual and definitional understanding of the words in the unit, having learned a number of words inside and out. He would also know how to figure out unknown words because his teacher would have modeled looking inside and outside of specific words to determine word meanings. And finally, D'Andre would have been more likely to apply the words correctly in his own speaking and writing, both inside and outside the school building.

Conclusion

Without question, vocabulary knowledge is critical to the academic achievement of middle and high school students. Knowledge of and about words not only serves as an excellent predictor of their achievement but is inexorably linked to overall reading comprehension and academic achievement. However, the enormous vocabulary demand on secondary students makes it impossible to provide direct instruction on each and every unfamiliar word they encounter. Instead, students need a combination of approaches that together foster vocabulary acquisition and lead to more sophisticated language use. The remainder of this book describes the components of an intentional model for vocabulary development across secondary content areas. With this approach, students become proficient readers, writers, and thinkers about the biological, physical, artistic, social, and literary world around them. In other words, the focus on academic vocabulary ensures their entrance into the wide world of knowledge.

2

Make It Intentional
A Framework for Selecting and Teaching Vocabulary

We're going to start this chapter with a few confessions. We didn't always teach academic vocabulary, and when we did, we certainly didn't teach words well. Looking back on this, guiltily, Doug recalls making a list of all the words students would need to know to be successful in his English class. He photocopied the list of words for students to learn and provided it to them at the beginning of the semester. As you can imagine, the list was a hodgepodge of words, including what we now recognize as general, specialized, and technical words. Doug recalls telling students that the words would appear regularly on quizzes, but he can't recall ever teaching the words or structuring class time such that students could engage in word study. Doug now realizes that he assumed that his high school students already had word-learning strategies and that they simply needed to be exposed to words in order to understand them.

Nancy also wants to confess. She remembers thinking that her middle school students should already know a lot of words and that she just needed to focus their instruction on the big words, especially those identified in the huge textbooks as important. "I used to orally define words that occurred in the textbook for students, thinking that this showed students that smart people know a lot of words," Nancy said, shaking her head at the memory. She also recalls thinking that the elementary school teachers who had these students before her should have done a little better job with vocabulary so that she didn't have to worry so much about it.

Thankfully, both of us required our students to read a lot. Wide reading probably saved their achievement. (We focus on this aspect of vocabulary development—extending academic vocabulary through wide reading—in Chapter 6.) But we have to ask ourselves how much better our students might have achieved had they experienced a combination of wide reading *and* intentional vocabulary instruction. Of course, this begs a whole new set of questions. Which words? What is the best way to teach the selected words? How do students become independent vocabulary learners? As Beck, McKeown, and Kucan (2002) remind us, we don't teach words just because they are *in* context, we teach words because students can learn *from* contexts.

Before we consider approaches to academic vocabulary instruction, we have to decide which words we should teach. As you might imagine, selecting words to teach has been a controversial matter.

▧ Selecting Words to Teach

Probably the most important question you'll be asked relative to academic vocabulary instruction is "Which words will you teach?" Once upon a time, our answer to this question was to focus on the words that students would encounter in their reading. This answer is faulty for a number of reasons, not the least of which is that this approach limits the range of words to those currently appearing in the books students are reading. Please don't misunderstand what we are saying—selecting vocabulary from a reading is useful and necessary. However, this approach to vocabulary selection, *when used in isolation*, is insufficient because it leaves too much to chance. Students need intentional instruction on a wider range of content words at their grade level than the text can possibly offer up, and it creates the false impression that reading the text is the best and chief forum for learning new words. Research shows that some words can be learned from reading, but not until students encounter the new words repeatedly—through reading many other texts, verbal discussion, and so on.

A sole focus on text-based word selection also fails to capitalize on all the books that students might want to read independently. That is, we don't teach words just because they're there. Consider Kaila, a junior in high school, who wants to be a child psychologist. If she were taught only words from the books she's currently reading in school, it's unlikely that she would spend much time in the world of words that interest her. Thankfully, her teachers know Kaila's goal and encourage her to learn words related to the biological world. One of her teachers gave her a copy of *The Illustrated Atlas of Human Anatomy* (Scientific

Student reading anatomy and physiology book

Publishing 2007), a collection of twenty-five anatomical charts containing more than three hundred illustrations and diagrams. He also showed her an interactive website that allows the user to move the cursor over human anatomical structures and provides a pop-up definition (www.innerbody.com/htm/body.html). Kaila was introduced to a host of words that weren't found in her current readings but would be useful as she organized her thinking about anatomy and physiology. Intentional vocabulary instruction involves keeping apace of our students' interests and improvising easy, authentic word learning to support their pursuits.

Narrowing the Possibilities by Sorting Words into Categories

Today, we're much more thoughtful in our answer to the question about word selection. Now, we think about the type of words that students need to know. As you no doubt recall from Chapter 1, words are often instructionally divided into three categories:

- *Tier 1, or General, Words*: Commonplace words that students typically learn from interacting with other people or from reading.

- *Tier 2, or Specialized, Words*: Words that have different meanings depending on the discipline in which they are used. These words are high frequency, meaning students will encounter them often in their reading. When students encounter a meaning of the word they aren't familiar with, they can get confused. Typically, students can define these words with easier words.

- *Tier 3, or Technical, Words*: Words that are specific to a content area or discipline. These words occur infrequently but can be barriers to understanding content (especially in middle and high school classrooms). Students typically do not know these words and have a hard time defining and using them.

LET'S TRY IT: ANALYZING A TYPICAL TEXT PASSAGE

Let's consider a typical text passage and identify the Tier 1, Tier 2, and Tier 3 words. This passage comes from a book commonly used in middle school history classrooms. It focuses on George Washington and the Revolutionary War. The opening three paragraphs read:

> On an October day in 1753, Robert Dinwiddie, Royal Governor of His Majesty's Colony in Virginia, sat in his office in Williamsburg, the capital of Virginia, reading the latest reports from the frontier. The French were causing trouble again, pushing their way into British land. There was a whiff of war in the air.
>
> Dinwiddie must have realized that Virginia's western boundary was fuzzy. Some Virginians even said that their colony stretched across the continent. But Dinwiddie knew that grand old claim was not realistic. He needed only turn to a map to see North America as it really was.
>
> Thirteen British Colonies stretched along the Atlantic Coast from New Hampshire to Georgia, with a long piece of Massachusetts land called Maine in the north and, south of Georgia, a small piece of land called British Florida. Spain held the rest of Florida, along with most of the land

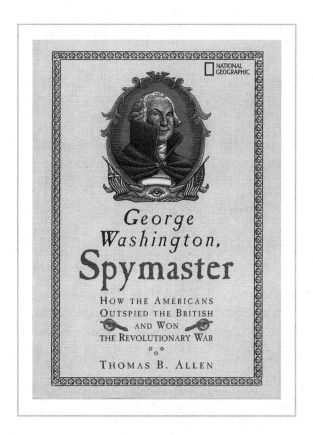

west of the Mississippi River. The French occupied land in the Mississippi Valley called Louisiana and much of the land north of the Saint Lawrence River. They called that possession New France. If the French kept expanding their hold, they could link their southern lands with New France. (Allen 2004, 1–2)

Of course there is no scientific way to identify specifically which words should be placed into the various categories. Typically, we put words in the general category if they are common enough that most of our students know them. We put words in the specialized category if our students can generally define them with terms that are less specific or if the words have multiple meanings that might interfere with understanding. And finally, we put words in the technical category when they are specifically aligned with the content under investigation. While this may differ slightly from the organizational system developed by Beck and her colleagues, it has worked for us in our efforts to focus on academic vocabulary in middle and high school classrooms. Using these lenses, we selected words from the George Washington passage and identified which tier they were in; see Figure 2.1 for our analysis.

General (Tier 1)	Specialized (Tier 2)	Technical (Tier 3)
whiff	office	Royal
war	capital	Governor
fuzzy	reports	Majesty
grand	frontier	Colony
realistic	western	continent
	boundary	
	claim	
	held/hold	
	occupied	
	possession	

Figure 2.1 *Selected words from* George Washington, Spymaster *(Allen 2004)*

As you can see, we did not include the proper nouns, such as the names of people, states, and countries. We assumed that students would have experience with these words based on the fact that they were in a history class. We'd also foreground reading this passage by having students look at a map so they would have a visual image of the locations being discussed as they read the passage.

THE SEMIFINALISTS: WORDS THAT MIGHT BE WORTH TEACHING

So which words did we focus on? Words that *might* need instructional attention. This simple analysis revealed fifteen words in the specialized and technical categories that are candidates for intentional instruction. That doesn't mean that we need to teach all fifteen of these words. We know that there is a limit to the number of individual words a student can learn in any given week. Scott, Jamieson-Noel, and Asselin (2003) reported students can be successfully taught eight to ten words in a given week. Given this, you want to narrow down the semifinalists to a manageable number of words. We know that this isn't an easy process, but we have identified a number of questions that we can ask ourselves to determine which words will receive instructional attention and which will not. We have developed these questions after analyzing the recommendations of a number of vocabulary scholars, including Graves (2006), Nagy

(1988), and Marzano and Pickering (2005). Figure 2.2 contains the topics we consider in selecting words as well as the questions we ask ourselves.

THE FINALISTS AND WHY WE CHOSE THEM

Based on the questions in Figure 2.2, we selected six words from the George Washington text to teach. From Tier 2, we selected *held/hold*, *occupied*, and

Topic	Questions to Ask
Representation	• Is the word representative of a family of words that students should know? • Is the concept represented by the word critical to understanding the text? • Is the word a label for an idea that students need to know? • Does the word represent an idea that is essential for understanding another concept?
Repeatability	• Is the word used again in this text? If so, does the word occur often enough to be redundant? • Will the word be used again during the school year?
Transportability	• Will the word be used in group discussions? • Will the word be used in writing tasks? • Will the word be used in other content or subject areas?
Contextual Analysis	• Can students use context clues to determine the correct or intended meaning of the word without instruction?
Structural Analysis	• Can students use structural analysis to determine the correct or intended meaning of the word without instruction?
Cognitive Load	• Have I identified too many words for students to successfully integrate?

Figure 2.2 *Considerations for selecting vocabulary words*

possession because these words are conceptually related and we know that this helps students transfer words into their knowledge base. In addition, these words were being used in very specific ways (related to history) that are not the ways in which they are commonly used. From Tier 3, we chose *Colony* and *continent*. These two words are essential to understanding early U.S. history. We believed that students would learn the roles of leaders (*Governor*, *His Majesty*) and about royalty in units of study that focused more specifically on these topics.

Of course, there is no one right answer to the specific words that you choose to teach from a reading selection. The choice depends, in part, on the point of the school year in which the reading occurs, the assessed needs of students, and the range of instructional materials students will come in contact with.

That said, we can generalize that systematic vocabulary instruction requires that teachers

1. know that *they* have to choose words—it's not a decision that should be left to textbook writers;

2. know from where to choose words; and

3. know how to categorize words in order to then winnow the possibilities of what to teach. This requires a decision-making model for selecting those big-bang-for-your-buck words that crack open key content understandings and that moonlight, so to speak, by helping kids infer meanings of many other words via common roots, prefixes, or suffixes. Words such as *judge*, *judgment*, *adjudicate*, and *judgmental* are some examples of these words.

A DECISION-MAKING MODEL TO FURTHER GUIDE YOUR SELECTION

When selecting your heavy hitters, it's helpful to evaluate the words you're considering from these vantage points:

- Is the word representative?

- Is it repeatable?

- Is it transportable?

- Is it best understood by students through contextual analysis?

- Is it best understood by students through structural analysis?

- Does it overburden the cognitive load?

Representation

This may be the aspect most frequently used by teachers when choosing a word for vocabulary instruction. Is the term representative of an important idea or concept? These words often come in the form of labels, such as *tectonic plate*, *patriot*, and *parallelogram*. At other times, it may be a gateway word for a series of related words. For instance, teaching *create* can lead to learning a number of variants, including *creator*, *creative*, and *re-creation*.

Repeatability

If the word is going to be used repeatedly, either within a unit of instruction or throughout the school year, it may be a good candidate for intentional instruction. Novel words that appear only once are not good choices because the learner won't receive multiple exposures to the word—a necessary condition of vocabulary learning (Stahl and Fairbanks 1986).

Transportability

A third consideration in selecting a word for instruction involves transportability. Is it likely that this word will be useful in another learning arrangement, such as a classroom discussion or written assignment? Words that are transportable may be useful in other content areas as well, such as *temperate*, which is used in English to describe an even-mannered character and in science to describe a mild climate.

Contextual analysis

This analysis requires looking at the context in which the word is used rather than viewing the word in isolation. If a term used in a reading is accompanied by surrounding words or phrases that define the word, then it is probably not necessary to provide direct instruction for this word.

Structural analysis

As with context, the structure of the word may be sufficient for your students to infer the meaning. This judgment requires that you know your students well and are familiar with their exposure to the prefix, root, and suffix in the word. For example, a civics teacher might decide not to explicitly teach *economic interdependence* because the affixes and roots present in this term are apparent.

Cognitive load

Unlike the other elements, consideration of cognitive load has less to do with the word itself and more to do with the learning context. At some point, the sheer number of words becomes daunting, and vocabulary instruction can detract from learning content—a bit like the tail wagging the dog. There aren't any hard-and-fast rules about what constitutes the right cognitive load, as it varies by learner and content. Our very informal rule of thumb has been to try to limit ourselves to two to three words per lesson, knowing that at some point students can't assimilate any more information.

Much in the spirit of that famous movie line "Show me the money," we imagine at this point you're saying to yourself, *Man, enough already, just give me the word lists!* You may even have flipped to the index, looking for a list or two. The temptation to dive into a word list is strong. Word lists convey a sense of completeness, especially when they are categorized by grade or content level. We find lists to be very useful, too, but only when balanced against an understanding of the types of words as well as a method for deselecting ones that are not needed. In other words, we use lists to inform our instruction, not formulate it. Keeping in mind the last few pages of discussion on types of words and a method for selecting words for systematic instruction will take you further in your teaching than any list, so thanks for hanging in there.

Using Word Lists to Inform Instruction

Who doesn't love a list? Getting to the end of one is a satisfying experience, be it a grocery, chore, or holiday gift list. David Letterman makes a top ten list every night he broadcasts. The same holds true for vocabulary word lists. Many of us may be familiar with ones commonly used by our elementary colleagues, such as the Dolch Sight Word list. This compilation of 220 words has been around for many decades and has been utilized in nearly every K–3 classroom in the country. We may envy our colleagues as they test students with flash cards and check off whether a child correctly names each word or not. Why isn't middle and high school vocabulary instruction so straightforward?

In truth, elementary educators rely on much more than the Dolch word list, and they struggle with the same kinds of issues we do. Which words to teach? What is the best method? The words they choose may have fewer syllables, but they are no less complex in nature. Let's examine three types of word lists: general academic terms, basic English words, and word-part lists.

ACADEMIC WORD LIST

By the time students reach middle school, grade-level word lists are less common, in particular because they are so heavily influenced by the nature of the content being taught. Instead, academic word lists are more useful because they highlight terms commonly used across content areas. These are composed mostly of Tier 1 and Tier 2 words.

One of our favorites comes from the work of Averil Coxhead of Massey University in New Zealand. She analyzed the running text of 414 textbooks from the major content areas and identified the most frequently used terms. She eliminated the first two thousand, as they consisted of sight words and other simple terms. She then applied further criteria regarding the range of texts in which terms appeared as well as their frequency, and clustered them by word families (Coxhead 2000). The resulting 570 most frequently used word families include words such as *data*, *procedure*, *response*, and *theory* and can be found at http://language.massey.ac.nz/staff/awl/awlinfo.shtml.

The Academic Word List can be sorted in a number of different ways, depending on the purpose. Colleagues at our school have used the list to identify terms used on tests and have incorporated these to strengthen students' test-wise strategies (Fisher and Frey 2008). Departments have worked together to locate terminology from the list used frequently in their own classes. In addition, because the words are arranged according to word families, teachers are able to extend student knowledge to related words.

OGDEN'S BASIC ENGLISH WORD LIST

Many of our students are new to English and are simultaneously challenged to learn English and learn *in* English (Fisher, Rothenberg, and Frey 2007). These learners need to acquire a tremendous volume of vocabulary in a short period of time. We were intrigued when we learned of a list developed in 1930 by Charles K. Ogden. His list began as a constructed language of 850 words that are phonetically regular and therefore easy to pronounce (see Figure 2.3). In addition, these words can be used in combination with others to form other words. For a time after World War II, the list was even touted as a universal language that could bring about world peace. While we haven't had quite that much success with it, Ogden's list has been a great tool for working with English learners who are new to the language.

WORD-PART LISTS

Vocabulary instruction should always look toward the ultimate goal, which is student independence, since it's a certainty that you won't be there every time students encounter an unfamiliar word. Students' ability to structurally analyze

Operations (100 words)

come, get, give, go, keep, let, make, put, seem, take, be, do, have, say, see, send, may, will, about, across, after, against, among, at, before, between, by, down, from, in, off, on, over, through, to, under, up, with, as, for, of, till, than, a, the, all, any, every, little, much, no, other, some, such, that, this, I, he, you, who, and, because, but, or, if, though, while, how, when, where, why, again, ever, far, forward, here, near, now, out, still, then, there, together, well, almost, enough, even, not, only, quite, so, very, tomorrow, yesterday, north, south, east, west, please, yes

Things (400 general words)

account, act, addition, adjustment, advertisement, agreement, air, amount, amusement, animal, answer, apparatus, approval, argument, art, attack, attempt, attention, attraction, authority, back, balance, base, behavior, belief, birth, bit, bite, blood, blow, body, brass, bread, breath, brother, building, burn, burst, business, butter, canvas, care, cause, chalk, chance, change, cloth, coal, color, comfort, committee, company, comparison, competition, condition, connection, control, cook, copper, copy, cork, cotton, cough, country, cover, crack, credit, crime, crush, cry, current, curve, damage, danger, daughter, day, death, debt, decision, degree, design, desire, destruction, detail, development, digestion, direction, discovery, discussion, disease, disgust, distance, distribution, division, doubt, drink, driving, dust, earth, edge, education, effect, end, error, event, example, exchange, existence, expansion, experience, expert, fact, fall, family, father, fear, feeling, fiction, field, fight, fire, flame, flight, flower, fold, food, force, form, friend, front, fruit, glass, gold, government, grain, grass, grip, group, growth, guide, harbor, harmony, hate, hearing, heat, help, history, hole, hope, hour, humor, ice, idea, impulse, increase, industry, ink, insect, instrument, insurance, interest, invention, iron, jelly, join, journey, judge, jump, kick, kiss, knowledge, land, language, laugh, law, lead, learning, leather, letter, level, lift, light, limit, linen, liquid, list, look, loss, love, machine, man, manager, mark, market, mass, meal, measure, meat, meeting, memory, metal, middle, milk, mind, mine, minute, mist, money, month, morning, mother, motion, mountain, move, music, name, nation, need, news, night, noise, note, number, observation, offer, oil, operation, opinion, order, organization, ornament, owner, page, pain, paint, paper, part, paste, payment, peace, person, place, plant, play, pleasure, point, poison, polish, porter, position, powder, power, price, print, process, produce, profit, property, prose, protest, pull, punishment, purpose, push, quality, question, rain, range, rate, ray, reaction, reading, reason, record, regret, relation, religion, representative, request, respect, rest, reward, rhythm, rice, river, road, roll, room, rub, rule, run, salt, sand, scale, science, sea, seat, secretary, selection, self, sense, servant, sex, shade, shake, shame, shock, side, sign, silk, silver, sister, size, sky, sleep, slip, slope, smash, smell, smile, smoke, sneeze, snow, soap, society, son, song, sort, sound, soup, space, stage, start, statement, steam, steel, step, stitch, stone, stop, story, stretch, structure, substance, sugar, suggestion, summer, support, surprise, swim, system, talk, taste, tax, teaching, tendency, test, theory, thing, thought, thunder, time, tin, top, touch, trade, transport, trick, trouble, turn, twist, unit, use, value, verse, vessel, view, voice, walk, war, wash, waste, water, wave, wax, way, weather, week, weight, wind, wine, winter, woman, wood, wool, word, work, wound, writing, year

Things (200 picturable words)

angle, ant, apple, arch, arm, army, baby, bag, ball, band, basin, basket, bath, bed, bee, bell, berry, bird, blade, board, boat, bone, book, boot, bottle, box, boy, brain, brake, branch, brick, bridge, brush, bucket, bulb, button, cake, camera, card, cart, carriage, cat, chain, cheese, chest, chin, church, circle, clock, cloud, coat, collar, comb, cord, cow, cup, curtain, cushion, dog, door, drain, drawer, dress, drop, ear, egg, engine, eye, face, farm, feather, finger, fish, flag, floor, fly, foot, fork, fowl, frame, garden, girl, glove, goat, gun, hair, hammer, hand, hat, head, heart, hook, horn, horse, hospital, house, island, jewel, kettle, key, knee, knife, knot, leaf, leg, library, line, lip, lock, map, match, monkey, moon, mouth, muscle, nail, neck, needle, nerve, net, nose, nut, office, orange, oven, parcel, pen, pencil, picture, pig, pin, pipe, plane, plate, plough/plow, pocket, pot, potato, prison, pump, rail, rat, receipt, ring, rod, roof, root, sail, school, scissors, screw, seed, sheep, shelf, ship, shirt, shoe, skin, skirt, snake, sock, spade, sponge, spoon, spring, square, stamp, star, station, stem, stick, stocking, stomach, store, street, sun, table, tail, thread, throat, thumb, ticket, toe, tongue, tooth, town, train, tray, tree, trousers, umbrella, wall, watch, wheel, whip, whistle, window, wing, wire, worm

Qualities (100 general words)

able, acid, angry, automatic, beautiful, black, boiling, bright, broken, brown, cheap, chemical, chief, clean, clear, common, complex, conscious, cut, deep, dependent, early, elastic, electric, equal, fat, fertile, first, fixed, flat, free, frequent, full, general, good, great, grey/gray, hanging, happy, hard, healthy, high, hollow, important, kind, like, living, long, male, married, material, medical, military, natural, necessary, new, normal, open, parallel, past, physical, political, poor, possible, present, private, probable, quick, quiet, ready, red, regular, responsible, right, round, same, second, separate, serious, sharp, smooth, sticky, stiff, straight, strong, sudden, sweet, tall, thick, tight, tired, true, violent, waiting, warm, wet, wide, wise, yellow, young

Qualities (50 opposites)

awake, bad, bent, bitter, blue, certain, cold, complete, cruel, dark, dead, dear, delicate, different, dirty, dry, false, feeble, female, foolish, future, green, ill, last, late, left, loose, loud, low, mixed, narrow, old, opposite, public, rough, sad, safe, secret, short, shut, simple, slow, small, soft, solid, special, strange, thin, white, wrong

Source: Ogden, C. K. No date. "Ogden's Basic English Word List—in His Order." http://ogden.basic-english.org/words.html

Figure 2.3 *Ogden's Basic Word List*

a word to identify its parts and then make an educated prediction about the meaning will serve them well. You use this all the time. For example, Doug has been studying about the brain and has encountered quite a volume of unfamiliar vocabulary. When he read the phrase *sagittal plane* (a term used to describe a view of the brain that goes through the center from front to back), he was initially confused. Where did that word come from? However, he quickly made a connection between the diagram and the word *Sagittarius*, the archer in astrology. He visualized an archer with his bow drawn back and then understood the derivation of the word. There are many websites featuring Latin and Greek roots, and most have been developed for middle and high school students. One of our favorites is sponsored by the Kent (Washington) School District and can be found at www.kent.k12.wa.us/ksd/MA /resources/greek_and_latin_roots/transition.html.

In addition to learning the derivational meanings of Latin and Greek root words, students benefit from understanding prefixes and suffixes (collectively called *affixes*). Teaching students the high-frequency affixes can equip them with the tools they need to deconstruct an unfamiliar word in order to understand it. For example, the prefix *un-* appears in 26 percent of all English words with a prefix, while the suffix variants *-s* and *-es* are featured in 31 percent of all suffixed words (White, Sowell, and Yanagihara 1989). A chart of the most common affixes appears in Figure 2.4.

So far, we have discussed the types of vocabulary, outlined a decision-making model for identifying words for possible intentional instruction, and shared examples of useful word lists. The final step in selecting words is through identifying words by department or course. This helps us ensure that students move through a sequence of courses with a growing base of vocabulary knowledge.

Selecting Technical Words by Department or Course

At many secondary schools, teachers in each department or content area are identifying technical vocabulary that requires instruction. Teachers meet in course-alike groups (e.g., all of the world history teachers) to identify essential terms and all agree to teach them during each unit of instruction. This approach is consistent with the curricular initiatives common to secondary schools, especially standards alignment and the development of pacing guides. By agreeing to teach specific technical academic words, instructors assure teachers of subsequent courses that students will arrive with grounding in the terminology. For example, it is useful for the tenth-grade biology teachers to know that the ninth-grade earth science instructors taught students Tier 2 words such

Rank	Prefix	Percent of All Prefixed Words	Suffix	Percent of All Suffixed Words
1	un-	26	-s, -es	31
2	re-	14	-ed	20
3	in-, im-, il-, ir- (not)	11	-ing	14
4	dis-	7	-ly	7
5	en-, em-	4	-er, -or (agent)	4
6	non-	4	-ion, -tion, -ation, -ition	4
7	in-, im- (in)	3	-able, -ible	2
8	over-	3	-al, -ial	1
9	mis-	3	-y	1
10	sub-	3	-ness	1
11	pre-	3	-ity, -ty	1
12	inter-	3	-ment	1
13	fore-	3	-ic	1
14	de-	2	-ous, -eous, -ious	1
15	trans-	2	-en	1
16	super-	1	-er (comparative)	1
17	semi-	1	-ive, -ative, -tive	1
18	anti-	1	-ful	1
19	mid-	1	-less	1
20	under- (too little)	1	-est	1
	all others	3	all others	1

Source: White, T. G., Sowell, J., and Yanagihara, A. (1989, January). Teaching Elementary Students to Use Word-Part Clues. *The Reading Teacher,* 42 (4), 302–308. Reprinted with permission of the International Reading Association.

Figure 2.4 *The twenty most frequent affixes in printed school English*

as *passage*, *dissolve*, and *concentration* as well as Tier 3 words like *acid, alkaline, capillary action, hydrologic,* and *osmosis* during the unit on water science. These terms and the related concepts are relevant to teaching about cell membranes, so the biology teachers are then able to make connections back to earth science, helping students understand that the movement of water shares common attributes whether it is moving through a valley or a semipermeable cellular membrane.

Two sources of information are useful for identifying department or course vocabulary. The first is the state content standards document, whose descriptions feature a large number of vocabulary terms. We often think of these documents as being written for an adult audience, but they can be a treasure trove of student vocabulary. For example, the first Algebra 1 standard for

California contains the following technical vocabulary terms: *symbolic reasoning*, *integers*, *rational and irrational numbers*, and *closure properties*. In addition, these specialized terms appear in the same standard: *calculations*, *central*, *identify*, *properties*, *operations*, *applicable*, *demonstrate*, and *assertions*. (Interestingly, several of these Tier 2 words appear on Averil Coxhead's Academic Word List as well.)

A second source for identifying vocabulary words is contained in the curricular materials themselves. The glossary and bolded words in the textbook are obvious choices for consideration, and most instructor materials also contain additional support materials for vocabulary instruction. It should be noted that we are discussing vocabulary lists from textbooks last. While they are a good source, they are not going to be very useful if merely photocopied and assigned to students to learn somehow. Effective vocabulary development requires careful and purposeful selection of words. It also requires that the instruction of vocabulary honors what we know about good teaching and learning.

■ Intentional Instruction of Selected Words

Given that this entire book is about how to develop academic vocabulary for secondary students, we'll resist the urge to tell you everything now. Instead, we will describe the instructional framework we use to foster word knowledge in our classrooms. This model doesn't depend on hours of instruction devoted to learning just a few words, but rather requires that vocabulary development become a natural part of classroom instruction. In other words, intentional instruction of vocabulary doesn't stand apart from the content—it is a necessary factor in content mastery.

Our framework for deliberate vocabulary instruction is based on a gradual release of responsibility model (e.g., Pearson and Gallagher 1983). In essence, the gradual release of responsibility model suggests that teachers move from assuming all of the responsibility to sharing responsibility with students to transferring responsibility to students. This release of responsibility occurs at the macro and micro levels as teachers plan daily lessons, units of study, and entire semesters and school years. In our work on vocabulary in middle and high school classrooms, both in our own classrooms and in schoolwide efforts, we have found three components of the gradual release of responsibility especially helpful: *demonstrations*, *practice with peers*, and *independent applications*. In addition, our work with entire school buildings suggests that a schoolwide vocabulary initiative can raise the level of word consciousness and create a much-needed focus on word learning.

Demonstrations: The Importance of Teacher Modeling

One component of the gradual release of responsibility requires that teachers demonstrate and model their own thinking and understanding. Teacher read-alouds, think-alouds, and shared readings are particularly effective ways for providing the modeling that students need. These approaches can be used to raise word consciousness, teach word-solving strategies, and foster vocabulary metacognition. They can also be used to demonstrate the importance of vocabulary in understanding texts. For example, consider the following passage from the book *World War II for Kids* (Panchyk 2002), which we read to a group of students:

> Franklin Roosevelt was an immensely popular president and the only one in history to serve more than two terms. Not only was he responsible for helping the United States get out of the Great Depression, Roosevelt was seen as a brilliant and optimistic wartime leader. His speeches raised hopes and helped inspire America to victory. (57)

There's quite a bit of content knowledge packed in those few sentences: they describe the amount of time Roosevelt spent in office, name two important contributions, and comment on his public persona. When Nancy read this to her students, she stated, "As I read that, I noticed how the author chose words that created a positive impression of this president. He used *immensely popular*, *helping*, *brilliant*, *optimistic*, *hopes*, and *inspire*. But I also know that he had many critics. I'm not sure they would use the same terms to describe Roosevelt. I've got a little bell going off in my head that reminds me that a good historian looks for more than one perspective." In a few sentences, Nancy showed her students how she grouped words conceptually, analyzed those words to reach a conclusion, and extended her thinking to model how an expert understands content material. She didn't need to hang up a banner that said, "Vocabulary Time." Instead, she incorporated vocabulary development seamlessly into her content teaching.

As part of the integration of career information into the English class, Doug was recently reading aloud an informational text to a group of high school students. The school had chosen the book *Ten Things I Wish I'd Known—Before I Went Out into the Real World*, by Maria Shriver (2000). Of course teachers model more than vocabulary; they also model comprehension, text structures, and text features, but words are an important part of understanding reading. After reading the following passage, Doug stopped to talk about the differences between *critical*, *judgmental*, and *jealous*.

So relax, take your time, and don't be in such a rush. And remember: No job is beneath you. But also know that on your way up, you may run into critical and judgmental people, jealous people—people who may say you got where you are because of who you are or what you are, what school your father went to or what you look like or who you knew when. No matter. Shake it off. If they have a problem with you, it's their problem, not yours. Just shelve your ego, put your head down, and bulldog forward, grinding it out. There is no better way to gain respect—and self-respect—than through hard work. (21)

As with most modeling opportunities, there are so many things that could have been said. In this case, Doug chose to focus on the differences between

Doug modeling while reading

some words that were strung in the same sentence. He said, "I love the message of this section: be yourself and work hard. I think that's great advice, sage advice as we've said before, not to pay attention to people who are jealous. I really like how she has lumped some personalities together: critical, judgmental, and jealous. They're different, of course, but they are similar. I think that critical can be good. We've talked about critiques of our work in this class and how it can have a positive impact when it's constructive criticism. The others, being judgmental and jealous, just get in the way of productive relationships." Given that this section came at the end of the chapter, Doug's students had a chance to focus on the words and the differences between the words as part of their peer practice, which followed Doug's modeling.

Peer Practice: The Importance of Consolidating

Building academic vocabulary through peer interaction is another component of our instructional design. We know it is not enough for teachers to model the use of vocabulary; students must have lots of opportunities to build their nascent knowledge using oral language. You can't be the arbiter of all that talk, so you'll need to structure lots of opportunities for students to work in peer groups. We know you're thinking that a cocktail party seems to break out each time you allow some peer talk in your classroom. We assure you that the strategies we discuss in Chapter 4 will at least result in talk that is on topic.

Oral language experiences are essential to the social and cognitive development of adolescent learners. These opportunities are even more critical for secondary students who are simultaneously learning English and learning in English (Fisher, Rothenberg, and Frey 2007). The intent of these interactions is to provide learners with a chance to clarify their understanding of new words, apply these words to new situations, and deepen their conceptual understanding by linking prior knowledge to new learning.

We know that students build their understanding of academic vocabulary through activities that cause them to discuss, clarify, and collaborate. Our experiences suggest that having students produce something as a result of their collaborative efforts results in increased use of academic vocabulary. The use of words with peers provides an opportunity for consolidation of learning. Accordingly, we regularly use semantic feature analyses and word maps. We also ask students to work together to develop concept circles, collaborative posters, and shades-of-meaning cards. We invite them to make predictions about readings using text impressions and to think aloud with one another as they engage in partner reading. The discussions that emerge from these interactions foster a deepening understanding of vocabulary and the related concepts under investigation.

Consider the conversation a group of students was having about the central nervous system. At the point that this conversation occurred, they had experienced a number of teacher read-alouds, watched a short film about the brain, and conducted lab experiments about motor neurons. The task for this particular day was to create a collaborative poster about one aspect of the central nervous system. One group worked on neurons while another group worked on the cerebral cortex, and still another worked on issues related to the brain stem. Listening in as the group focused on neurons completed its task clearly demonstrated the students' use and understanding of academic vocabulary.

Andrew: But I don't get it. Where do those dendrites go?

Melissa: They're just floating out there in brain space, kinda like floating in liquid, but being supported by the neuroglia cells.

Andrew: But how do they know what to connect to?

David: They're always searching for connections to other neurons. When they do connect, they can establish a pathway. Then the impulse can travel from neuron to neuron.

Melissa: See, this is 2-D [*pointing to the poster*], but you have to think 3-D. The dendrites hook up with the terminals from other cells so that the neurotransmitters can cross over and make the nerve fire.

David: And when they fire over and over, that pathway gets reinforced so that the cells are more likely to stay connected with each other. Well, not connected because they don't really touch, but they stay near each other to receive the signal.

Andrew: And it only goes one way, so that the dendrites don't also have to send the message the other way, right?

Melissa: Exactly!

The conversation these students had demonstrates their collective ability to integrate academic vocabulary, both specialized and technical, into their thinking. In using and discussing these terms, students build their understanding of both the content and the words used to discuss the content. If students are not provided these opportunities to negotiate with their peers, learning becomes a passive activity in which words are held in the air of the classroom, but not in the minds of the learners.

Independent Activities: The Importance of Application

At some point, students need time to apply what they have learned through teacher modeling and peer collaboration by consolidating their understanding of the vocabulary. We want individuals to utilize writing in order to strengthen their own command of the language. As we explain in Chapter 5, activities such as word sorts and A–Z charts encourage students to group and categorize concepts. Students also use words in generative sentences, journal writing, and paragraph frames. In addition, they need to further develop their metacognitive awareness about how they learn words, so they assess their knowledge using vocabulary self-awareness techniques and develop vocabulary cards based on Frayer's model (Frayer, Frederick, and Klausmeier 1969) when they need more formal study techniques.

Once again, these individual activities can be integrated into the content instruction of the classroom. For example, academic vocabulary development in the geometry classroom is embedded into journal writing when the teacher invites his students to use *base*, *bisect*, and *volume* to explain how a problem is solved. It is at this stage, in individual activities, that teachers should assess students' vocabulary knowledge. Simple assessments requiring students to use

Student working on vocabulary journal

words can provide teachers with information about which students have mastered the vocabulary and which require additional instruction.

■ Word Consciousness: The Importance of a Schoolwide Focus

Vocabulary demand in middle and high school far exceeds the capacity of any teacher or school to directly teach each word, and yet many students seem to acquire a rich vocabulary that outstrips the amount formally presented. These learners are able to accomplish this through extensive reading. The incidental academic vocabulary learning that takes place when a reader is engaged with a text that is not too difficult can range from anywhere between five and fifteen new words out of every one hundred unknown ones (Nagy and Herman 1987). Students need repeated exposures in authentic contexts to really understand a word. Wide reading provides this exposure as students read a variety of texts and genres. It's a numbers game, really—the more print material students come in contact with, the more exposure they have to familiar and unfamiliar vocabulary. Over time, they acquire new words and deepen their understanding of partially known ones.

Chapter 6 focuses on two well-known initiatives for increasing reading volume—sustained silent reading (SSR) and independent reading. SSR has gained popularity in secondary schools because of its effects on student motivation, interest, and academic achievement (Fisher 2004). It is typically designed as a fifteen- to twenty-minute daily period when students and teachers read materials of their own choosing, including nonacademic texts. This is often accomplished through a schoolwide initiative because it transmits the values of a school regarding reading and provides support for teachers who do not traditionally use a lot of reading material in the classroom. For example, an art teacher participating in a schoolwide SSR program has a broad range of reading materials located in the room such as newspapers and donated books. She augments her collection with art-related texts like comic books and reviews of local art shows.

Many teachers also incorporate independent reading of content-related texts in their classes. The amount of information derived from print is increasingly essential in middle and high school classes, and students need time to process this information. (Most of us have learned by this time that telling them everything just doesn't work.) Independent reading sometimes includes textbook passages, but it is an ideal time to expose students to richly varied materials—after all, the textbook isn't the syllabus, and publishers are the first to tell you

that no single textbook could contain all the information needed for any subject. Independent reading is commonly done in English, history, and humanities classrooms, but it is equally viable in other courses as well. Opportunities for independent reading include gathering information for essays and research projects, as well as extensions of topics that have been taught. For example, the physics teacher can assign independent reading of chapters from *Guinea Pig Scientists: Bold Self-Experimenters in Science and Medicine* (Boring 2005) and then ask students to explain the physics behind scientists' attempts to perfect jet pilot safety gear and protection from extreme heat and cold.

Conclusion

It isn't enough to merely present students with a list of words for them to memorize and regurgitate on the next quiz; they must be taught in a systematic and intentional way. This doesn't mean that content instruction must be pushed aside to make room for vocabulary, but it does mean that the two need to be consolidated so that word learning is a natural and necessary part of learning the content. The first step is to identify the general, specialized, and technical vocabulary necessary for each content area. This is best done in course-alike collaborations with fellow instructors. An added benefit to this approach is that other educators are aware of what their students are learning.

In order for academic vocabulary development to be systematic and intentional, students need an instructional design that provides them with varied experience with words. This includes

- modeling by the teacher to raise word consciousness and show students problem-solving approaches to figuring out unfamiliar words;

- building academic vocabulary knowledge through peer interactions;

- consolidating academic vocabulary through individual activities; and

- extending vocabulary and conceptual knowledge through wide reading.

Taken together, these strategies help students become word wise and content rich.

Make It Transparent
Teacher Modeling of Academic Vocabulary Learning

3

Nayeli enters her algebra classroom and sees a couple of problems on the board. They are unfamiliar to her; they have a number of operations in different parentheses. The first problem reads: 17 − (10 − 3). Nayeli's teacher, Ms. Rojan, turns to her class, smiles, and jokes, "Don't panic, I'll walk you through it. Easy as pi." The students laugh at her well-worn joke, and their tension eases.

Mrs. Rojan thinks aloud each as she solves the problem:

> Hmmm, the first thing I see is that the order in which the arithmetic is done may change the result. I have to pay close attention here. I remember that expressions within a pair of parentheses—those curved lines that surround numbers or words that look like rounded brackets—are to be computed *before* expressions outside the parentheses. I also know that without parentheses to show what calculation is to be done, multiplications and divisions are to be done before additions and subtractions. Multiplication and division are said to have a higher priority; they're more important in the solving. So for this first problem, if I ignored the parentheses . . . see these little lines here [*pointing to the parentheses*], I would say, "Seventeen minus ten is seven, minus three is four." *But*, if I followed the correct order of operations and first subtracted three from ten and got seven and then subtracted seven from seventeen, my answer would be ten. That's the correct answer because I know the importance of these parentheses.

"Are you with me?" she asks her students. They nod their heads. So far, so good. The second problem reads $[8(x+1)+2](\frac{3}{2} \times 2)^2$ and Nayeli's teacher explains her thinking about how to solve this problem as well, outlining each step in solving the problem and the reasoning behind each step.

In some middle school classrooms, teachers tend to put a new kind of problem on the board and invite their students to swan dive into the deep end of the pool—to do the problem independently—and then begin instruction after students struggle with it for a bit. Some teachers put a problem like this on the board and then ask students a series of questions about the problem, an approach that tends to make the advanced math students shine but undermines the confidence of other students. Instead, Ms. Rojan believes the most effective instructional move is to model her thinking using the academic vocabulary of a mathematician. For example, to start she said, "I see that the innermost parentheses can't be reduced further. $X + 1$ is in the *innermost*, the most inside parentheses, and I know that I can't add terms that aren't alike. So, next I look to the *outside* and need to distribute the eight across the terms inside the parentheses. By *distribute*, I don't mean pass out papers, I mean apply it across the terms, so inside the brackets, I would get $(8x + 8) + 2$."

Nayeli's teacher continued to model her thinking about this problem until it was solved. She then picked up the book she was reading aloud to the class,

Word learning in geometry

A Gebra Named Al (Isdell 1993), and began reading. In this part of the book, the characters are in a cave, which is symbolic of parentheses:

> Julie found herself in another small chamber, like the first they had entered. "What's this?" she demanded. "Aren't we supposed to be in a large cave?"
>
> "You always start from the innermost Parenthesis," Al reminded her.
>
> "Oh, right," Julie remembered. "You start at the innermost, do all the math there, and work outward. At least, that's what you were supposed to do with a math problem." (40)

Ms. Rojan pauses and shares her thinking. Again, she explains her understanding of the order of operations and focuses on the role that the parentheses play in determining the correct answer. Mrs. Rojan often uses the first fifteen minutes of class in this manner, for she knows that students then go into the task with all her language and all her actions buzzing in their heads as they problem solve. A plethora of research supports Ms. Rojan's approach.

▪ The Importance of Modeling

Humans have a profound ability to mimic what they see others say and do. This innate ability has served our species well for tens of thousands of years; it's how we learned to communicate and how we transmit information from one generation to the next. Through observations of others—our parents, for example—we acquire certain behaviors. As we observe others, we incorporate their models into our behavior. Who can forget the toddler who mimics her mom's harried search for the car keys or the way she talks to a friend on the phone? We remember an episode of *America's Funniest Home Videos* in which a young boy was "golfing" in his backyard. His mother asked, "Can you golf like Daddy?" Immediately, the child slammed the golf club to the ground and yelled "Damn it!" Yes, that's how Daddy plays golf.

Of course, most of the behaviors we incorporate into our patterns are more adaptive than our father's golfing performance. Just think back on all the things in your life you've watched another person do before you tried it on your own—skiing, playing tennis, using chopsticks for the first time. Most of us have vivid memories of learning to ride a bike or a parent patiently (or not!) teaching us how to drive a car. But learning to read? We might have a few flickering memories of pretend reading, phonics lessons in first grade, but then it's kind of a fast forward to full-tilt reading of *Charlotte's Web* or *The Exorcist*! What happened in between? Alas, reading isn't a physical behavior. It's a cognitive one, a thinking task, and as such it is invisible to others. As a result, we cannot directly demonstrate it. We have to talk about it. As Duffy noted, "The only way to model thinking is to talk about how to do it. That is, we provide a verbal description of the thinking one does or, more accurately, an *approximation* of the thinking involved (since there is no one way to do any reading task)" (2003, 11).

This is what Nayeli's teacher did. She provided her students an approximation of the thinking required to solve problems using the correct order of operations. She did so by sharing her own thinking, explaining her thinking, and making an invisible process more transparent for her students. Over time, Nayeli incorporated the thinking, procedures, and habits modeled by her teacher. On one afternoon, we heard Nayeli say to a peer, "I can't just tell you the answer. Let me talk you through it. I can explain my thinking about this problem to you." Let's look at two other teachers modeling their thinking.

Mike Ford's world history students were studying early Chinese civilizations when he shared with them Confucius' comments on ways to promote a good government in China. The words Mr. Ford read, attributed to Confucius, included:

> If the people be led by laws, and uniformity be imposed on them by punishments, they will try to avoid the punishment, but will have not sense of shame. If they be led by virtue, and uniformity be provided for them by the rules of propriety, they will have a sense of shame, and will become good. Let the ruler be filial and kind to all people; then they will be faithful to him. Let him advance the good and teach the incompetent; then they will eagerly seek to be virtuous.

After reading the passage, Mr. Ford explained his thinking. "So, if I understand this correctly, Confucius believed that people will attempt to avoid punishment when laws are enforced, but that there was a better way of creating a society. He wanted people to make decisions because of their beliefs, their virtues, and the virtues of society. I can infer that he wanted to help people make decisions about how to act because it was right and not because they were afraid of being punished. But his recommendation about how a ruler should act is a bit confusing to me. He says to be *filial* and *kind*, and that doing so will ensure that people are faithful. So, from the context, I predict that *filial* is a positive trait, but I'm not sure what it really means. I also can't really take the word apart to understand it, so I think I'll google it and find out a bit more about being filial. It sounds like it's an important concept for Confucius."

Similarly, physics teacher Avery Justice shared a piece of text with her students related to light and monitors. The text read:

The ability of the three electron beams (red, green, and blue) in a CRT monitor to meet at a single point and produce one dot is called convergence. If a monitor is mis-converging, you will notice shadows of blue or red around any white images. Often, this will occur in only some parts of the screen. Some CRT monitors have convergence controls, but most do not, making it impossible to correct this condition without opening it up, which isn't a good idea due to how CRT monitors hold electrical energy. (geek.com)

Ms. Justice shared her thinking and understanding about this piece of text with her students and modeled her understanding of the three beams meeting in one place. She focused on the target word *convergence* and said, "There are great examples of convergence in this text, but I'm not sure that the word is really well defined. When I see the word *convergence*, I notice that it starts with *con-*, which I know means *with*. I also know that *verge* is a boundary or edge, like being on the verge of tears. I also remember that the suffix *-ence* is an action or process. So, it's a bit clunky, but the word *convergence* means that there is a process in which two or more things come together to an edge or boundary or fixed point. And that fits with the text, so I'll read it again with this deeper understanding of the word."

Of course, good teachers have always modeled to facilitate learning. Modeling has been used to improve student behavior (Wilford 2007), facilitate inquiry in science (Jablon 2006), and teach students how to have literature discussions (Farris, Nelson, and L'Allier 2007). Expert teachers know that modeling is a critical phase in developing student independence. Expert teachers also know that modeling alone is insufficient to change achievement (Fisher and Frey 2008). Students need opportunities to apply what they've seen modeled as well as receive feedback on their attempts, and they need time to consolidate their understanding.

We want to give modeling bigger billing than it has received in other books on vocabulary, because our students do so much better when they've heard and watched us identify and solve unknown words and can then mimic our *procedures* for discerning meaning. We've got to get away from the mindset that academic vocabulary instruction is about teaching specific words. Rather, it's about teaching specific strategies for approaching all words, and remembering that the more we talk about and express an excitement and curiosity about new words, the more our students will absorb this attitude and bring it to bear in their own reading and writing (Bromley 2007). And finally, we need to model when and how to consult resources when our word-solving strategies fall short.

Interestingly, there is some concern about modeling as a component of vocabulary instruction. For example, Beck, McKeown, and Kucan suggest that modeling "can be useful, but teachers should use it sparingly because it puts students in the passive role of overhearing the teacher thinking aloud" (2002, 41). They continue, suggesting that modeling be reserved for times in which students are being introduced to the idea of gaining meaning from context or when complicated or subtle context is being used. They recommend that students "be made part of the deriving-meaning process as soon as possible, queried along the way as meaning elements are derived from context" (41).

We understand this concern, and we are also concerned that some teachers may think they are modeling but they are merely explaining word meanings. We have also seen good modeling that simply went on for too long! When kept brief, five to ten minutes, as part of a systematic approach to vocabulary development, modeling is a powerful instructional component. Our classroom experience and research with middle and high school students indicate that modeling, when used to establish word-solving procedures to determine meaning and not teach specific words (e.g., Fisher, Frey, and Lapp in press; Lapp, Fisher, and Grant 2008), is a powerful way to develop academic vocabulary.

Our own recent research is anchored in a body of research on modeling and thinking aloud that suggests that modeling our thinking processes is a critical phase of instruction (e.g., Afflerbach and Johnston 1984; Bereiter and Bird 1985; Davey 1983; Wilhelm 2001). Simply asking students questions about words, especially in a whole-class format, is unlikely to ensure that all students learn to use new vocabulary. The one or two students participating in the back-and-forth dialogue with the teacher are probably learning, but what about the other thirty-five students in the class? Essentially, they fall into the passive role that Beck and her colleagues (2002) noted.

Again, for content area teachers, it is so tempting to teach specific words and keep moving forward, covering that curriculum. But in the end, this shortcut fails us because our students wind up dependent on us, and they flounder in the reading we assign because we haven't given them the mental models for solving unknown words *while engaged with texts*.

■ Modeling Procedures for Solving Words

We have organized teacher modeling of word-solving strategies into three components: context clues, morphology and word parts, and resources. In each of these cases, we look inside Nayeli's classrooms for examples.

Context Clues

One of the ways that readers figure out unknown words is through the use of context clues. This is an example of an outside-of-the-word strategy. The goal of modeling context clues is to provide students with enough examples so that they can use this approach independently. Of course, context clues don't work 100 percent of the time, and students need examples of when this approach fails and what else they can do. Before we consider when to use context clues, let's note when they don't work.

In their study of basal reading programs, Beck, McKeown, and McCaslin (1983) identified four categories for natural contexts. Of these four categories, some are helpful and others are not. The continuum of contexts they identified spans from misdirective to nondirective to general to directive. *Misdirective* contexts are those in which the reader would assume an incorrect definition from the words surrounding the target or unknown word. For example, in the following sentence, readers might assume that *anchorite* was someone who liked being around people and not that it means a person who lives in seclusion, usually for religious reasons. The words around the unknown word convey a different message and are therefore misdirective.

> It's hard to imagine James was an anchorite. He's so full of life and love of people. He often is the last to leave a party.

Alternatively, a *nondirective* context clue is of little or no assistance to the reader. These clues fail to help the reader make meaning. For most readers unfamiliar with the terms *loquacious*, *melancholy*, and *pococurante*, the context in the following sentence doesn't help the reader understand the words.

> Jessica seems to change based on her environment and whom she's with. She can be loquacious, melancholy, or pococurante.

General context clues provide readers with some information, but not a level of detail that would allow them to identify specific nuances or connotations of the target word. Readers of the following sentence have a sense that *ambled* means to have moved slowly. They may not understand that the word more specifically connotes an unhurried or leisurely walk and that the author is playing with the word because *ambled* is also used to describe an easy gait, especially that of a horse.

> Justin ambled to the stable, not at all in a hurry to get himself on another horse.

And finally, the type of context clue that really helps the reader is a *directive* one. These clues provide readers with information that they can use to determine the target word's meaning, and even the nuances of the word. Consider the word *gauche* in the following sentence. Readers unfamiliar with the word will easily sense that the writer has chosen a word that conveys distaste and lacking social polish.

> Joan's behavior, licking the spoon, telling toilet jokes, and criticizing the food during dinner, is tacky, crude, and even vulgar, to the point of being gauche.

Given that there are so many context clues that don't work, it seems reasonable to add a note of caution about spending too much class time trying to teach students to use context clues. Or rather, we must balance it with teaching them how to determine *if* the context clues are going to help them; sometimes our weaker students get trapped in erroneous meanings because they think context clues will always work. When you consider that our students are reading widely, seeing all kinds of words in different contexts, then it becomes clear we have to teach them how to muddle through all kinds of idiosyncratic contexts, some helpful, some not. As Beck, McKeown, and Kucan (2002) asserted, we don't want students to learn words only *in* context; we

Physics teacher modeling word solving

need to teach them how to learn words *from* context. There are a number of texts, especially informational texts and textbooks, in which authors purposefully embed words in context to help readers comprehend. As such, the use of context clues should not be left to chance, and this is where teacher modeling comes in. Modeling the five ways in which authors provide context clues helps students develop their skill in using context to discover words and their meanings.

1. *Definition or Explanation Clues*: The most obvious clue occurs when the author explains the word immediately after its use. For example:

   Access to clean water would ameliorate, and improve upon, living conditions within the village.

2. *Restatement or Synonym Clues*: Sometimes authors provide a restatement or synonym of a challenging word. For example:

   Access to clean water would ameliorate living conditions within the village such that life would be tolerable for the people who live there.

3. *Contrast or Antonym Clues*: Some clues provide a contrast for the target word such that reader can infer the word's meaning while reading. For instance:

   Access to clean water would ameliorate living conditions within the village, whereas continued reliance on a polluted river would exacerbate a bad situation.

4. *Inference or General Context Clues*: Sometimes a word or phrase is not immediately clarified within the sentence. Relationships that are not directly apparent are inferred or implied. The reader must look for clues before or after the sentence in which the word is used. For example:

   Access to clean water would ameliorate living conditions within the village. Clean water would make life tolerable because residents could focus on other pressing needs such as finding food and shelter.

5. *Punctuation Clues*: Readers can also use punctuation and font style to infer word meanings. Quotation marks (showing the word has a special meaning), dashes, parentheses or brackets (enclosing a definition), and italics (showing the word will be defined) all help readers determine what the word means in the given context.

   Access to clean water would ameliorate—make tolerable—living conditions within the village.

Let's consider the impact that teacher modeling of context clues has had on Nayeli. We've already seen how her algebra teacher defined unfamiliar vocabulary while solving a problem and reading from a text. Of course, teacher modeling with texts is not limited to vocabulary work; teachers also model comprehension and text structures. Although in this book, we focus on the vocabulary examples that teachers provide their students, it's important to note that the teachers we quote did not limit their modeling to vocabulary; they also explained their use of comprehension strategies. For example, Nayeli's English teacher read aloud from Chapter 5 of *Firegirl*:

> I'm talking about having an election in class. Just like the real political elections coming up in a few weeks, in which I hope your parents will vote, I'd like to have a little mini-election right here. An election for classroom president. (Abbott 2006, 24)

Pausing, the teacher commented, "I appreciate how the author reminded me about the word *election*. I know from this sentence that he's using the word to mean the voting process and not a class, like my favorite elective is music. I also like the connection he makes between what the class will do and what their parents do—they vote in an election."

Over the next several pages, additional words about elections are used, including *government*, *public office*, *primary*, *candidates*, *nominate*, and *committee*. For each of these terms, Nayeli's teacher explained her thinking and how she used the context of the passage to understand the words. She knew that these words would come in handy for the social studies class and that they were words students would need to know in the future as involved citizens. But more importantly, here was an opportunity to model the use of context clues, especially context clues that worked.

Nayeli's science teacher, reading aloud from the text *Extreme Weather* (Farndon 2007), which was projected onto a screen by a document camera, noticed the word *hailstones* and read aloud the passage that explained them. In doing so, he pointed out the way that the author defined *hailstones* in the text.

> Thunderclouds don't just rain down drops of water. They drop balls of solid ice called hailstones, too. They are typically as large as peas, but sometimes as large as apples. Hailstones form in thunderclouds because the clouds are so tall that the upper levels are very cold, and so turbulent that they can hold an ice ball aloft. (39)

Following the reading, Nayeli's science teacher noted his appreciation that the author "helped out by very clearly explaining the word *hailstones*. I'm sure that I could have taken a guess by looking inside the word. I know what hail is, we have that, and I know what stones or rocks are, but the context helped me realize that there weren't really small rocks in the hail, but rather they were larger pieces of hail that form specifically in thunderclouds."

Teachers should also point out when context clues fail to help the reader. While reading Al Gore's (2007) book *An Inconvenient Truth* to a student government class, the teacher noted that sometimes context clues fail. Here's the passage from the text:

> The documentary film *March of the Penguins* was a surprise hit in 2005. However, the movie neglected to point out that the population of emperor penguins is thinning.
>
> Since the 1970s, the penguins' neighborhood has become increasingly warm. The Southern Ocean experiences natural shifts in weather from one decade to the next, but this warm spell has continued, causing the thinning of sea ice. Less sea ice means fewer krill, the penguins' main food source. Also, the weakened ice is more likely to break apart and drift out to sea, carrying off the young penguin chicks, who often drown.
>
> Is global warming responsible for the thinning of the penguin population? Scientists believe so. (94)

After reading aloud this passage, the teacher paused and wondered aloud about the word *thinning*: "I'm not sure that I'm correct about this. I know that the word *thin* can mean skinny and not fat. That definition works for the ice—it got skinnier and was more likely to break. But I'm not sure that it applies to the penguins. First, I see the picture, and they don't look thin to me. Second, I'm not sure that the former vice president would care about skinny penguins. I have to find out how else the word *thinning* can be used."

Morphology and Word Parts

In addition to looking outside words for clues about their meaning, students need to look inside words to determine meaning. Providing examples of how to use morphology and word parts ensures that students will apply this strategy on their own. We're using morphology here in the linguistic sense, to mean the smallest meaningful units of language. For example, adding *-s* to the end of many words adds meaning (more than one), as when *dog* becomes *dogs*. But morphology is more complex than that. Teaching students to look inside words for their morphology and word parts requires a fairly sophisticated knowledge of the language. Figure 3.1 identifies five aspects of morphology and word parts that teachers must be aware of if they are to be able to model this inside-the-word approach to determining word meanings. In addition, Chapter 2 contains a table with the most common suffixes and prefixes (see Figure 2.4).

Like context clues, word parts don't always illuminate meaning. For example, there are a number of false cognates that result in misunderstandings. Consider, for example, the word *embarrassed*. It sounds a lot like the Spanish word *embarazada*, which means pregnant. You certainly wouldn't want to confuse these two terms! Whereas *religion* (English) and *religión* (Spanish) mean more or less the same thing, *fabric* and *fábrica* do not (*fábrica* means factory). Figure 3.2 contains a sampling of the many common Spanish and English cognates useful in school. There are a number of resources on the Internet for false cognates and we encourage you to take a look at them, using key words such as Spanish cognates, Latin cognates, or false cognates.

Nayeli's teachers also used morphology and word parts in their modeling. Remember the teacher who was reading aloud from Al Gore's book? When he got to page 120, on which the words *destructive* and *deterioration* occur, he said, "*De-* is an interesting prefix. It means from, down, and away and generally suggests a reversal or removal. That helps me understand the word *destructive*—things being deconstructed, destroyed. It also helps me understand *deterioration*. I know that the root, *-terior*, is related to a geographical area, like

Component	Definition	Example
Prefix	A word part (affix) added to the beginning of a root or base word to create a new meaning	*hyper-* meaning over, as in *hyperactive*
Suffix	A word part (affix) added to the end of a root or base word to create a new meaning	*-est* meaning comparative, as in *tallest*
Root or base	A morpheme or morphemes to which affixes or other bases may be added	*port* meaning to carry, as in *transportation*
Cognates	Two words having the same ancestral language and meaning	*Rehabilitation* and *rehabilitación* meaning to restore or improve
Word family	A group of words sharing a common phonic element	*Judge, judgment, adjudicate, adjudication*

Figure 3.1 *Morphology and word parts*

territory, and also words like *posterior* and *anterior* meaning locations. I also know that *-tion* is a process or action. So, deterioration means that there is a place that is in the process of removal."

In another case, Nayeli's science teacher came across the word *carnivore* while reading and said, "I remember that *carne* is a Spanish word for meat, as in *carne asada*. The suffix *-vore* focuses on eating. So I can easily figure out that a carnivore is a meat eater. That's different from *herbivore*, which I remember because *herb* is a plant. It's also different from *omnivore*. *Omni-* means everything or all, so an omnivore eats both plants and meat."

The English teacher also noted instances when looking inside a word improved understanding. Sometimes Nayeli's teachers played with the words they were reading simply as a reminder of the process of using word parts and morphology. For example, while reading *Firegirl*, the teacher read the sentence

English	Spanish
action	acción
affection	afección
application	aplicación
circulation	circulación
civilization	civilización
classification	clasificación
direction	dirección
election	elección
elevation	elevación
evaporation	evaporación
fiction	ficción
function	función
identification	identificación
infection	infección
investigation	investigación
multiplication	multiplicación
nutrition	nutrición
position	posición
revolution	revolución

Figure 3.2 *English and Spanish cognates*

"The skin was all rough and uneven" (Abbott 2006, 33) and said, "Uneven, not even. I don't think this means odd, as in odd numbers: one, three, five, seven, nine. I think that the author really does mean not even, not flat, not smooth. It seems that Jessica's face was really damaged pretty seriously from the burns."

Resources

When the first two systems—context and word parts—fail, teachers model the use of resources. These take readers even further outside the word to determine meaning. Commonly, teachers use peer resources, dictionaries, and the Internet in their modeled quests for figuring out word meanings.

As an example, let's return to the student government class reading Al Gore's book. When he wasn't sure that his context clues for *thinning* worked, the teacher clearly indicated that he needed more information. Consulting an online dictionary, he read aloud a variety of definitions for the word *thinning*. At first, he found a number of definitions that focused on trees and removing some trees to provide growing space for better-quality trees, and removing dead or dying trees to reduce pest problems. Applying this definition aloud for his students didn't work. He then found a definition that worked—reducing a population—and said to the class, "I think I've got it. Yes, the former vice president would be worried about this, as am I! The ice is getting skinnier, but the penguins are getting fewer and fewer in number. The word *thinning* works in both cases."

Nayeli's science teacher modeled using a peer when he called the teacher next door to ask about the word *cirrostratus* as it was presented in the sentence "Soon, the blue sky begins to fill up with milky veils of cirrostratus clouds, formed lower down on the front" (Farndon 2007, 36). The teacher next door replied on speaker phone and described a very interesting type of cloud, one that is "almost transparent with a whitish veil of fibrous, almost hairlike, appearance. These clouds usually totally cover the whole sky and often produce a halo phenomenon. These clouds are made of ice crystals and are thin. These clouds are in high altitudes, usually between twenty thousand to forty thousand feet" (Wikipedia).

Thanking his colleague, the science teacher added, "I'm never embarrassed to ask a friend about a word. Now I know the word and can help another person—pay it forward, I say. I want to find this kind of cloud and see what else it offers."

■ Conclusion

Modeling is good first teaching. In fact, our experience and research suggests that it is critical teaching. Simply said, students need—deserve—models of strategies they can use in their own reading. That's not to say that modeling is sufficient, in and of itself, as an instructional intervention. Modeling must be part of a larger academic vocabulary initiative in which students are provided opportunities to build, consolidate, and extend their word knowledge.

Modeling should not take significant amounts of time away from content instruction; vocabulary *is* content instruction. You would be hard-pressed to find an expert lawyer, biologist, or chief financial officer who did not know the words of his discipline. Our middle and high school classrooms would become much better places of learning if we could discontinue the false dichotomy between content and literacy. Using words is how experts across disciplines communicate with one another. Our job as teachers is to welcome students into these conversations.

Make It Useable

Building Academic Vocabulary Through Peer Talk

4

Maurice and Francisco trade conspiratorial whispers in their tenth-grade world history class. They and their classmates are pairing up to devise games that will help one another prepare for the final exam. Ms. Schaeffer, their teacher, has used a variety of games to reinforce key vocabulary terms since the beginning of the year, so her students are well versed in the formats of bingo, *Jeopardy*, *Who Wants to Be a Millionaire? Hollywood Squares*, Balderdash, Scrabble, *Wheel of Fortune*, and *Password*.

Maurice and Francisco are designing a category game based on the old *$25,000 Pyramid* show to help their peers shore up their understanding of ancient Greece. To pull this off, they have to determine the key understandings in the Greek unit the class completed; these will be the hidden categories on the game board (see Figure 4.1). The players will have to name these categories (e.g., art, philosophy, science) based on the examples they are given. Maurice and Francisco have compiled a list of possible examples for each category, which took quite a bit of discussion, negotiation, and reviewing of the unit. These boys know the examples they offer up to classmates must represent the category well or the game won't be fair—or fun to play (see Figure 4.2).

"We need more contributions to science," says Francisco. The boys flip through a pile of materials from the unit and begin rereading and skimming.

"Hey, here's one. I forgot about siphons," Maurice says. "Let's add that to the list." Francisco admits that he doesn't remember what a siphon is. "It's like when you take a tube and suck some air out of it so you can get water to go

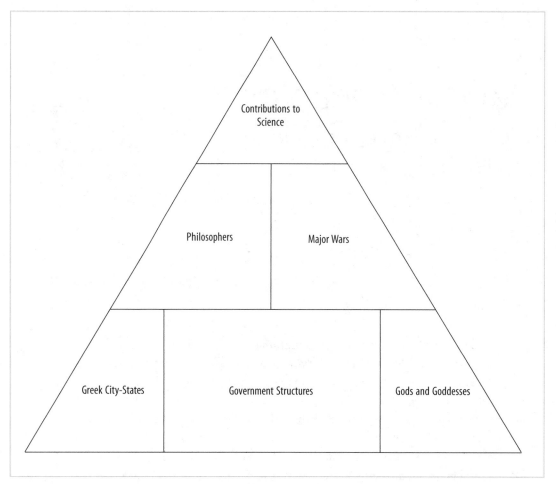

Figure 4.1 *Pyramid game on ancient Greece*

from one bucket to another," Maurice explains. "It's how hydraulics work." Ms. Schaeffer, who has been listening in on partner conversations, smiles to herself. The vocabulary development that accrues from a student conversation like this one is the real McCoy; the actual playing of the game is the icing on the cake. She loves hearing the excited tone in students' voices and the confidence they exude when they explain their reasoning and new knowledge.

■ The Importance of Oral Language

Vocabulary doesn't exist only as an academic skill to be tested through multiple-choice items. It is a dynamic aspect of our daily speech, and it helps define how

Greek City-States	Government Structures	Gods and Goddesses	Philosphers	Major Wars and Battles	Contributions to Science
Pylos	oligarchy	Nike	Thales	Persian	measuring the Earth
Corinth	tyranny	Apollo	Plato	Marathon	charting the stars
Ithaca	monarchy	Persephone	Socrates	Peloponnesian	
Thebes	representative democracy	Artemis	Aristotle	Thermopylae	diving bell
Athens	direct democracy	Atlas		Trojan	Hippocratic oath
Sparta		Hermes			siphon
		Athena			
		Zeus			

Figure 4.2 *List of clues for the pyramid game*

others perceive us. Vocabulary can work against us—those who are too wordy are called *verbose*, while others who lack the verbiage to express themselves clearly are labeled as *inarticulate*. Our speech differs from written language as well. It is punctuated with social markers that reveal our cultural and class origins, our gender, as well as our experiences. Clichés and colloquial expressions, the presence or absence of profanity, even the extent to which we ask questions in a conversation disclose our identity to others. Our relative ability to use vocabulary with precision is not something that is limited to the school day; we carry our vocabulary with us every moment of our lives.

The language of young children gives us insight into vocabulary development. A toddler who has just learned *dog* labels every four-legged beast this way, be it cat, horse, or elephant. Over time, she acquires more labels and can discern the difference between a dog and a cat. Still later, she possesses the vocabulary of *beagle* and *poodle*. If she grows up to be a dog breeder, she'll correctly identify a Rhodesian ridgeback and a Portuguese water dog.

There's something happening to fuel this development, something that cannot be forgotten in the classroom: Academic vocabulary development doesn't come about only through listening. Yes, listening is important (as we discussed in the previous chapter). But listening is only one side; speaking is the other. To develop language, the child must engage in conversation with others who shape her understanding of concepts, correct her errors, and give her new labels to use. The vocabulary she develops over time comes in part from the opportunities she has to use vocabulary in spoken language. She then carries the oral language awareness into her reading and writing experiences.

■ The Evidence on Oral Language and Vocabulary Development

Now, for the bad news: Our teaching doesn't reflect what we know both intuitively and through the research about the benefits of talking to learn. Almost three decades ago, Watson (1980) noted that the discourse in secondary classrooms is dominated by teacher-led discussions that limit participation to a handful of students. Not much has changed since then.

We want to be clear here: Discourse is great when it's a true, classwide exchange. It's a vital element to content learning, as evidenced by the national standards in nearly every subject. What's askew is that in most middle and high school classes, the teacher *dominates* the spoken language, asks questions occasionally, and is answered by the same few students (Cazden 2001). So much potential language and academic development are lost in this unfortunate state of affairs, for adolescent oral language development and vocabulary acquisition are strongly linked. One study of eighth-grade mathematics students found that students taught to use heuristic vocabulary in their work with one another improved their mathematical learning, and the effect was even greater for lower-achieving students (Koichu, Berman, and Moore 2007). (Here's a bit of vocabulary development: *heuristics* in math are problem-solving approaches such as *make a graph*, *confirm the prediction*, and *keep track of calculations*.)

In another study, researchers investigated the language gains made by first- and second-language learners in an undergraduate psychology course that featured small-group discussion. Importantly, both groups (first- and second-language learners) improved in their vocabulary and content learning as a result of the discussions they had with peers (Burger and Chretien 2001). It seems that small-group oral language activities that target vocabulary development are useful. A comparative study of high school students enrolled in a first-year world language course found that those who constructed word maps with peers acquired more new vocabulary than those who did not use the mapping activity (Morin and Goebel 2001).

But conversations involving academic vocabulary don't just break out in the classroom, whether they be among the whole class or small groups.

Students have to be taught to have these conversations. And you have to create a culture in the classroom where pursuing word meanings is fun and where it's OK to be in the dark about a word. Let students know when you don't know a word that you came across in your reading outside of school, and let students know you love it when they speak up about a word they don't know. Celebrate it and pursue the answer together, right on the spot if at all possible. And when you can, invite your English language learners to provide insights about a vocabulary word's equivalent in their native language.

■ Characteristics of Productive Group Work

As you know, fostering meaningful work between partners or in small groups is more complicated than simply throwing students together and assigning them a task. It is useful to consider these characteristics of effective peer learning (Johnson, Johnson, and Smith 1991).

- *Positive Interdependence*: The activity should necessarily require the participation and contribution of all members of the group and cannot be done by one member. Lack of participation by any member would diminish the likelihood that the task can be completed successfully.

- *Face-to-Face Interaction*: Never underestimate the power of personal connections between students, especially when the intent is the development of language. Communicators need face-to-face interaction in order to communicate.

- *Individual and Group Accountability*: This is undoubtedly the most common complaint among teachers and students when group assignments are mentioned. The solution is an easy one but is usually overlooked. Every member needs to be held individually accountable. A group grade in the absence of individual accountability is a surefire recipe for unrest. Our solution? Require all participants to use different ink colors and sign their names accordingly. The evidence of everyone's contribution is instantly apparent.

- *Interpersonal and Small-Group Skills*: Just because they are in middle or high school doesn't mean students know how to work well with one another. Establish your rules of engagement and teach them. Our rules include the following:
  1. Listen as an ally.
  2. There is value in every voice.

Students engaged in production group work in geography

3. If you have a disagreement, try to solve it together.

4. If you can't resolve it, talk to the teacher.

- *Group Processing*: Students need time to discuss their work together. In a busy secondary classroom, it's easy to push this component aside. Make a habit of building a few minutes into the end of the activity to allow participants to discuss the process they used.

■ Three Tips for Successful Peer Interactions

We always believe in stacking the deck in the favor of the teacher, and peer collaboration activities are no exception. We have found that when we are clear on the purpose of the activity, when we are deliberate in varying the vocabulary enrichment activities, and when we integrate the activities into content learning, the success rate accelerates.

Tip 1: Provide Students with a Purpose Statement

Adolescents are sensitive to busywork. The moment they decide that you've given them a task to keep them busy and buy yourself some peace, you're going to have some understandable civil disobedience—mostly in the form of complaining! But when you establish a clear purpose with students and link it to their overall mastery of the content, they'll get on board. This is different from giving directions, which merely list a sequence of steps. Purpose provides students with a model of metacognition so that they recognize a path to learning. In our many visits to classrooms, we have found that establishing a clear purpose is the most neglected instructional design element. We often ask students a simple question: "How do you know when you're done?" If the answer is "When the teacher tells me" or "When the bell rings," we know that no clear purpose has been established for that learner.

Write a purpose statement for your students that includes three components: First, tell them the *outcome*. (By the end of this activity, you and your partner should be able to describe the characteristics of plant and animal cells.) Second, tell them how the task relates to their *content mastery*. (An objective of this unit is that you are able to compare and contrast these types of cells and explain how they reproduce.) Third, tell them how they will *measure success*. (You'll know you've done this correctly when you are able to explain the differences to one another without using the graphic organizer you've developed.) We've developed a habit over the years of posting the purpose on the board as well as saying it orally.

Tip 2: Remember That Variety Is the Spice of Life—Especially for Adolescents

Variety is especially important when it comes to academic vocabulary development. Secondary students satiate quickly on any one particular vocabulary activity, so we've found it helpful to get into the mindset of offering up a few different types of peer activities each week. Graphic organizers are great, but not if they are used five days a week. It is a fine balance between establishing habits of work and allowing students to habituate to too few vocabulary activities. Rotating effective vocabulary learning strategies, such as the ones outlined in this book, will ensure that students remain focused on the instruction provided.

Tip 3: Integrate Vocabulary Activities into the Content Flow

As much as possible, avoid activities that isolate academic vocabulary from the conceptual understandings of the unit of study. The goal of any activity should center on the necessary use of the vocabulary to complete the task. You won't find activities in this book that have students endlessly looking up dictionary definitions and mindlessly copying them onto worksheets. Nor do we ask students to write contrived sentences containing targeted vocabulary words. We learned our lesson the hard way years ago when we received this assignment from Edgar:

1. *Stoic* is a word.
2. *Narcissism* is a word.
3. *Draconian* is a word.

And so on—you get the idea. Choose activities for peer interaction that rely on the verbal and written use of vocabulary that is contextually bound. Words serve as the proxy for a multitude of concepts and ideas. You'll find that both academic vocabulary and content knowledge are built together.

■ Oral Approaches to Building Academic Vocabulary

Peer interaction activities that develop academic vocabulary primarily through oral language are a match made in heaven, because for students of this age, social interaction is key. The overarching goal of these activities is to compel students to integrate Tier 2 and Tier 3 vocabulary into their spoken communication. Think of this as verbal composition; the likelihood that students will use this vocabulary in written work increases as they become more comfortable with the syntactical and semantic demands. Of course, the conversations that students are having with one another should contain the words you've selected. In addition, students will likely need to draw on their developing knowledge of specialized vocabulary to engage in conversations with their peers.

Partner and Group Discussions: Noticing and Clarifying Understanding

PARTNER DISCUSSIONS

Discussions with a partner are ideal for creating immediate opportunities for students to integrate new vocabulary into their oral language. In addition, they are easy to implement because they don't require materials or the movement of furniture. The most well-known partner technique is *think-pair-share* (Lyman 1987), first conceived as a cooperative learning arrangement but quickly recognized for its value in allowing students to notice what they know and don't know and to seek clarification. This activity is implemented in three parts, beginning with a question that is posed to students ("What are some of the necessary characteristics of a *nocturnal* animal?"). Students are instructed to think about their response for a minute or two (a timer works best), then share their thoughts with another student ("They would need to be able to see in the dark or to use other senses like hearing and touch to locate food."). Finally, the teacher elicits responses from the class ("Let's hear from some of you about characteristics of *nocturnal* animals."). Short or incomplete responses can be scaffolded by the teacher to ensure that academic vocabulary is used in front of the entire class. For example, when Justin reported that "nocturnal animals have good eyes," his teacher scaffolded the response for the whole class by saying, "Yes, well-developed eyes and auditory adaptations are common with nocturnal animals."

Another worthwhile partner discussion activity is *turn to your partner and . . .* , often recorded in teacher lesson plan notebooks as *TTYPA*. As with think-pair-share, a well-crafted question will bring forth richer responses, so we are sure to plan questions in advance. These are great for planting vocabulary within group discussions. For instance, the science teacher continued the conversation about nocturnal animals by saying, "Turn to your partner and explain the advantages *nocturnal* animals have over *diurnal* animals. Be sure to use both those terms in your discussion." These prompts lower the risk for some learners who are reluctant to speak in front of the entire class, including some adolescent English language learners who may be feeling self-conscious about their language skills. By walking around and listening in on the conversations that partners have, the teacher knows which students use the terms correctly and which students need further instruction.

SMALL-GROUP DISCUSSIONS

Managing groups of three or more gets to be a bit more complicated, so procedures really pay off. A variation of think-pair-share, called *think-pair-square* (Kagan 1989), works well. The first two steps are the same, with students discussing a question in groups of two. On the teacher's signal, the partners then turn to another set of partners to confer. This is especially popular with teachers of mathematics, who use this strategy to foster discussion among students on explaining how and why a problem is solved using a specific algorithm.

The use of oral composition is good preparation for more formal written work (Dykstra 1994). When students have a chance to make meaning by talking with a peer, they are more likely to have fodder for writing tasks. For example, the group of students talking about nocturnal animals was asked to summarize their understanding following the conversation. Melody wrote the following after the group conversation, which provides evidence of key vocabulary terms that were intentionally taught:

> Nocturnal animals sleep during the day and are awake during the night. This behavior is the opposite of the common diurnal human lifestyle. Nocturnal animals have highly developed senses, especially of hearing, smell, and eyesight. These adaptations ensure their survival and provide advantages in terms of feeding and escaping the desert heat.

Group conversations can be useful for sharing information read individually by members of the group. In addition, the opportunity to retell reinforces the use of new vocabulary and concepts. The jigsaw method of small-group discussion is completed in two stages (Aronson et al. 1978). Students work first in an expert group of four members, with the shared goal of understanding a section of text. They read and discuss the main ideas and the supporting details with one another, asking questions to clarify their understanding. Once the members of the expert group are satisfied that they are comfortable with the information and can report it accurately, each returns to a second group of four, called the home group. The home group is composed of a representative from each expert group. Together, the four members of the heterogeneous home group share the information they learned in their expert groups. Members of the home group take notes and ask questions, seeking to synthesize the information. For example, Ms. Elliott established four expert groups for a jigsaw discussion of plate tectonics in her earth science class:

- strike-slip faults

- normal faults

- reverse faults

- thrust faults

Students worked in groups of four to read and discuss information about their assigned fault, then returned to a home group of four to share and learn about each type of fault. Ms. Elliott gave each student a note-taking guide called a conversational roundtable (Burke 2002) to foster recall (see Figure 4.3). Using the jigsaw process, students received multiple exposures to new vocabulary: reading, questioning and discussion, listening, retelling, and writing. Of course, they had to use both inside-the-word and outside-the-word strategies that had been modeled for them by their teacher in figuring out unknown words.

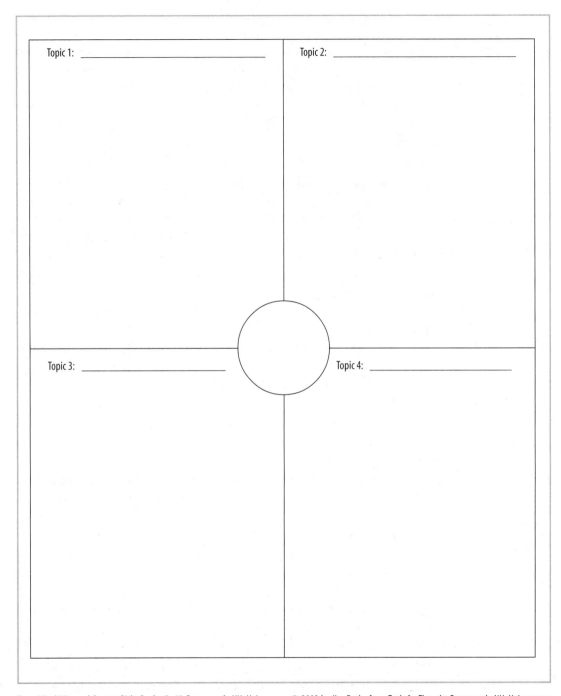

Topic 1: _____

Topic 2: _____

Topic 3: _____

Topic 4: _____

From *Word Wise and Content Rich, Grades 7–12*. Portsmouth, NH: Heinemann. © 2002 by Jim Burke from *Tools for Thought*. Portsmouth, NH: Heinemann.

Figure 4.3 *Conversational roundtable*

Student Think-Alouds: Modeling for Peers

In Chapter 3, we made a case for the importance of teachers modeling their thinking for students. Of course students can also think aloud—that is, model—for one another. There is a strong evidence base for the use of peer think-alouds. We know, for example, that student think-alouds improve comprehension (Baumann, Jones, and Seifert-Kessell 1993). We also know that student think-alouds provide peers with alternative models for understanding texts as well as authentic examples of academic vocabulary being used to understand (Oster 2001; Wilhelm 2001).

Students in middle and high school classrooms don't automatically know *how* to think aloud or even *what* to think aloud. Before asking students to engage in think-alouds, teachers must instruct them in how to do so. This instruction should provide examples and nonexamples of the type of talk expected during partner or small-group think-alouds. In our experience, students need to be reminded that these are not discussion groups (the previously described approach), nor are they read-alouds. In fact, we insist that students do not read the text aloud. They read the text individually in small chunks, and then one student shares his or her thinking with the group. They continue this process until the text is completed. In doing so, the group members have opportunities to listen in on each other's thinking.

Naturally, student think-alouds can be used in any content area. It's easy to imagine a small group of students each sharing their thinking as they read about the industrial era, child labor laws, friction and motion, or Georgia O'Keeffe's style of painting. But as a more detailed example, let's take a look at Ms. Neufield's English classroom. The students are focused on literary devices and how authors use words to establish tone and mood. Groups of students are reading different texts and Ms. Neufield is joining different groups to listen in on their think-alouds. She knows which students she really wants to hear, as this is part of her formative assessment system. By noticing how students think about texts, and the academic vocabulary they use to explain their thinking, Ms. Neufield determines which of her students need additional instruction and which of her students are meeting standards and expectations for the grade level.

Ms. Neufield joins the group reading *The Monkey's Paw* (Jacobs 1902). It's Justin's turn to share his thinking. Justin has difficulty expressing himself in large groups and Ms. Neufield knows that this practice and the feedback he receives from his peers will help him become more comfortable speaking in front of others. The group members read the first part of the text (see Figure 4.4). When they finish, Justin starts talking.

> WITHOUT, the night was cold and wet, but in the small parlour of Laburnam Villa the blinds were drawn and the fire burned brightly. Father and son were at chess, the former, who possessed ideas about the game involving radical changes, putting his king into such sharp and unnecessary perils that it even provoked comment from the white-haired old lady knitting placidly by the fire.
>
> "Hark at the wind," said Mr. White, who, having seen a fatal mistake after it was too late, was amiably desirous of preventing his son from seeing it.
>
> "I'm listening," said the latter, grimly surveying the board as he stretched out his hand. "Check."
>
> "I should hardly think that he'd come to-night," said his father, with his hand poised over the board.
>
> "Mate," replied the son.
>
> "That's the worst of living so far out," bawled Mr. White, with sudden and unlooked-for violence; "of all the beastly, slushy, out-of-the-way places to live in, this is the worst. Pathway's a bog, and the road's a torrent. I don't know what people are thinking about. I suppose because only two houses on the road are let, they think it doesn't matter."
>
> "Never mind, dear," said his wife soothingly; "perhaps you'll win the next one."
>
> Mr. White looked up sharply, just in time to intercept a knowing glance between mother and son. The words died away on his lips, and he hid a guilty grin in his thin grey beard.

Source: Jacobs, W. W. 1902. *The Monkey's Paw*. New York: Harper and Brothers.

Figure 4.4 *Excerpt from* The Monkey's Paw

The mood here is odd. But that's not the best word, I guess. I think that I'd pick the word *foreboding*. [*Ms. Neufield smiles at him.*] The words the author uses, like starting with the word *without* and then says things like *unnecessary* and *provoked*. I also think the beginning is foreboding because of the strange interactions the family is having. I'm intrigued by the comparison between the chess game and the visitor who's coming to the house. I don't know who's coming, but the words make me think that it will be important. I guess that this is the *foreshadowing* because the father stopped talking, even when he was mad, when he witnessed the look between the mom and son.

Justin continues, sharing his thinking for a few more minutes before turning to the group for comments. Heather, a member of the group, agrees that the mood is foreboding and says, "I like that you picked up on the word *provoked*. I think that the author put that word there very carefully. He wants us to notice this, that the family is aroused emotionally."

After a short discussion in which members of the group have a chance to ask Justin questions and comment on his thinking, they individually read the next section. Now it's Brian's turn to share his thinking. Ms. Neufield moves to the next group, pleased with the discussion she has witnessed. She notes that her students were thinking like literary critics, as evidenced by their use of the technical academic language she had introduced. She is also pleased that her students were able to ask questions, civilly, of one another about their thinking using specialized vocabulary.

The success of this peer work was based on a lot of practice. Ms. Neufield had modeled these respectful behaviors many times, and she had conducted think-alouds of her process of solving unknown words by using inside-the-word and outside-the-word strategies. Through good old trial and error, she'd come to realize that students did their best work when she explicitly required they use specific academic language in their conversations with one another. Earlier, she left it to chance and hoped the words would bubble up naturally, but they hadn't. As with each of these activities, you'll find your own ways of making them work well for your particular students.

Reciprocal Teaching: Structured Conversations

Reciprocal teaching is a discussion technique that requires students to use specific comprehension strategies in conversations with their peers. Following are the four specific comprehension strategies used in reciprocal teaching (Palincsar 1987):

1. *Summarizing*: The goal of the summary is to identify the major points presented by the author. The person responsible for summarizing the text reads the text with the purpose of getting the gist.

2. *Questioning*: The person responsible for this component identifies specific questions that the group can talk about. Questions can range from those whose answers can be found right in the text to those that require conjecture and personal connections.

3. *Clarifying*: The person responsible for clarifying attempts to clear up any confusions that the group has. To start, this student notes words or ideas that might be confusing and asks members of the group for ideas. The clarifier is not expected to have all of the answers but is expected to facilitate the conversation. Of course, other members of the group can ask for clarifications also.

4. *Predicting*: The person responsible for predicting makes an educated guess about what might come next in the text. The predictions should be plausible and realistic and should generate interest in reading the next section.

After reading a selection of text, students engage in a discussion. Typically, groups of four students have this conversation so that each student has something to contribute. One student summarizes, another questions, another clarifies, and the fourth predicts what might come next. During each reading, students take turns and rotate through each of the four comprehension components. The text is chunked or parsed, either by the teacher or by the group of students, and they stop at predetermined times while reading to discuss what they have read. Over time, and with practice, students begin to incorporate these four comprehension strategies into their independent reading (Oczkus 2003).

As you've probably figured out by now, we're interested specifically in the impact that this instructional routine has on academic vocabulary development. Imagine a group of students engaged in a structured conversation such as one based on reciprocal teaching. One of the components is clarifying, so students naturally talk about words that are confusing to them. Most often, they clarify technical words using either inside-the-word or outside-the-word strategies. That's the obvious impact that reciprocal teaching has on word knowledge. But think about the other components. When students summarize, question, and predict, they have to use all kinds of vocabulary: general, specialized, and technical. To talk about something they're reading requires that they use the words provided in the reading. Thus, this instructional routine is one more way that teachers can ensure students *use the words* and build their academic vocabulary.

Consider the opportunities reciprocal teaching provided students in a family and consumer sciences class. We had a chance to observe a group of four students reading a magazine article about trans fat. We asked the four members of the group what they knew about trans fat before reading, and they didn't know much. They noted that New York City had recently banned trans fat in restaurants and that "trans fat is bad for you." When asked specifically, "What is trans fat?" no member of the group could answer with more than "A type of fat." During the reading of the magazine article and the reciprocal teaching discussion they had, the students in this group experimented with a number of new ideas and new words. Some of the words they wrestled with were specialized terms. For example, in their article, *energy* was used in a scientific way (e.g., "the ability to do work") and did not mean active. They also explored the idea of *saturated* and how their understanding of the word fit with saturating the oil with hydrogen. While clarifying, the group discussed the idea of *shelf life* and what that term meant. Stacey said, "I like the idea of shelf life. It makes sense to say that something can only be on a shelf for so long before it has to be thrown away. I think that manufacturing ways to increase shelf life is the problem."

Bradley playfully added, "If you ask my last girlfriend, my shelf life wasn't sufficient."

In addition to the specialized words, the students in this group used a number of technical, content-specific words, including *rancidity*, *hydrogenated*, *oxidation*, *coronary heart disease*, and *cholesterol*. As evidence that they used these words in their discussions, consider the following excerpt from their conversation about the reading:

Michael: I have to summarize one of the most disgusting things I've ever learned. The whole idea behind trans fat was to reduce rancidity. Foods that would have rotted were saved a little while longer by using hydrogenated oils.

Stacey: I have a question. Why can't the scientists successfully remove trans fat from the Oreo cookie? It might reduce the shelf life, but it would also reduce the cholesterol levels.

Bradley: I predict that we're going to read more about coronary heart disease, but I don't understand why they call that it. Doesn't *coronary* mean heart? Isn't it like saying *heart* heart disease?

As we have noted, structuring conversations such that students in middle and high school classrooms can build their academic vocabulary is critical. If these students had simply been asked to define these terms, in the absence of an interesting reading and a peer discussion, we're not sure that they would have incorporated this information. Again, it's about the opportunities we provide students to use the words of the discipline.

■ Visual Approaches to Building Academic Vocabulary

Academic vocabulary learning is strengthened through visual displays of information. These have been found to be particularly effective when it is the student, rather than the teacher, who generates the visual display (McCagg and Dansereau 1991). Sometimes called *knowledge mapping*, these strategies allow students to position vocabulary in physical space in order to represent conceptual relationships. However, students do not have time to create visual representations of all the words they need to know. Word selection is critical. Choosing words that are worth it, as discussed in Chapter 2, is one of the most important things teachers can do in preparation for building academic vocabulary through visuals.

Word Maps: Making Connections Visible

There is a significant body of research that suggests that graphic organizers facilitate student learning (Ives 2007; Robinson 1998). Explanations for this increased learning focus on the fact that graphic organizers provide learners with visual representations of the content at hand (Fisher 2001). Graphic organizers also help students become more active readers in that they have a task to complete as they read (Alvermann and Boothby 1982). When graphic organizers correspond with the text structure, they help students clarify connections and relationships between concepts and ideas found in their reading (Fisher and Frey 2007). As a profession, we've known this for a long time.

But our focus here is on academic vocabulary development. And unfortunately, the ways that graphic organizers are often used actually impede vocabulary development. Graphic organizers are an opportunity for students to think, in words, about the content. They provide students an opportunity to organize information, again in words and sometimes images, in a way that helps them understand and remember. When well-meaning teachers simply copy a blackline master of a graphic organizer, the teacher, and not the student, has done the thinking. When well-meaning teachers who have heard that graphic organizers are helpful complete a graphic organizer on the overhead while members of the whole class add words, an opportunity is lost.

Looking through the lens of academic vocabulary development, we can see that the power of graphic organizers lies in their ability to facilitate conversations among students. Students need to be taught a number of types of graphic organizers and then be encouraged to use an appropriate graphic organizer to visually represent information (again, almost always with words). A list of common graphic organizer types can be found in Figure 4.5. Additional examples can be found at www.edhelper.com.

To appreciate graphic organizers in action, let's turn to a discussion a group of tenth-grade students were having about the causes and effects of World War II. The group had selected a vocabulary word map (e.g., Rosenbaum 2001), which is especially effective for helping students engage with and think about new terms or concepts in specific ways. (Other small groups used a time line and a compare-and-contrast chart. The key is the conversation that occurs as students complete the task, for that's when academic vocabulary gets bandied about and refined by peers.)

The group using a vocabulary word map was focused on the term *Axis Powers*. Here are a few of the comments made by group members as they constructed their map:

Paul:	So the Axis Powers are the bad guys?
Hunter:	I think it'd be more accurate to say that the Axis group started the invasions. They didn't see themselves as bad. We see them as bad because they declared war.
Jacqueline:	They invaded other countries. Way back in 1940, the Nazis invaded Netherlands, Belgium, and Luxembourg.
Hunter:	Yeah, and before that Germany invaded Poland and annexed Danzig.
Paul:	What does that have to do with the Axis? An axis is the center of something, right?
Jacqueline:	Yeah, they wanted to be the center around which other things revolved. The Axis Powers started in Germany, with the political party called the Nazis. Today we think of the Nazis as a radical, evil group, but they were a political party.
Paul:	OK, so the Axis Powers is really Germany and the Nazi party. They started the war by invading, right?
Jacqueline:	Yes, and then Italy got involved and became part of the Axis Powers. It wasn't Germany, but Italy who declared war on France and Britain. That's when the Axis Powers came into play.
Hunter:	But not power, as in strong or like in physics—doing work. The idea of a world power, a group that could influence the way the world worked, the world events of the day. So, here, in what it is, we should write something about power in this way.
Jacqueline:	And here, we should name all of the Axis Powers. It says here that Germany, Italy, Japan, Hungary, Romania, Bulgaria were the Axis Powers.
Paul:	So the others were the Allies, what they were not? That can go here?

In this brief excerpt, it's striking to see how this group of students used general, specialized, and technical vocabulary, isn't it? Notice how they incorporated the words they'd met in textbooks and heard from their teacher into their conversations. They clarified ideas and made connections with one another as they negotiated the task of creating the vocabulary word map. Again, the power is in the conversation, not the organizer. Students need multiple opportunities such as this to build their academic vocabulary with their peers.

Type	Description	Example
Venn	Overlapping circles that illustrate similarities and differences between two concepts	
Web	Central word or phrase linked to supporting labels, concepts, and ideas	
Sequence/process	Shows series of steps	
Chart/matrix	Rows and columns in table format that shows relationships vertically and horizontally	
T-chart	Two-column table for grouping ideas into categories	
KWL chart	Three-column chart for recording what is *known* about a topic, what students *want* to learn, and later, what they have *learned* about the topic	

Figure 4.5 *Common graphic organizers*

Semantic Feature Analysis: Exploring Relationships Between Words

Another specific type of graphic organizer is the semantic feature analysis. It's a matrix of sorts. Using this tool, students can examine related concepts (words) and make distinctions between them. We know that semantic feature analyses facilitate comprehension and engagement (Pittelman et al. 1991). We also know that this tool is a powerful way for engaging students in world learning (Stahl 1999). In working on the distinction between words, ideas, and categories, students use academic vocabulary, both specialized and technical. The key for us is to get students talking about the categories, persuading one another whether or not a characteristic applies.

It's easy to see the value of students building their academic vocabulary using semantic feature analysis by visiting Jeff Bonine's biology class. Mr. Bonine focuses a great deal of instructional attention on cells, parts of the cell, cellular life, and so on. At one point in his course, students complete a semantic feature analysis chart comparing plant and animal cells. Mr. Bonine explained, "They really need to see the differences between these two cells. I have them evaluate illustrations, but I want students talking about the differences. And I want them to record the differences for later reference. Along the way, I want students to become comfortable with the scientific vocabulary."

Using the tool found in Figure 4.6, students met in groups and debated the answers with one another. Here's a part of the conversation one group had:

Javier: They both gotta have a membrane. That's what keeps them together, all of the other stuff inside. Without that membrane, the nucleus would be rolling around in space. And the cell couldn't sustain itself. It needs a membrane to exist.

Hector: Yeah, it's like the film said, a cell is like a little room. Remember, it was named after the little room that the monks lived in. They didn't need a lot of room 'cuz they was working all the time.

Maria: OK, so both have cell membranes. That must mean that both have cell walls, right? I mean those monks had walls, so the cells must have walls, too.

Hector: But not chloroplast. They both don't got that. Remember that *chlor-* means green, so that's gotta be for the plants only, right?

It's clear that these students need continued work on their biology vocabulary relative to plant and animal cells. It's also obvious that they have

Component	Plant Cells Only	Animal Cells Only	Both Plant and Animal Cells	Neither Plant nor Animal Cells
Cell membrane	O	O	+	O
Cell wall	+	O	O	O
Chloroplast	+	O	O	O
Cytoplasm	O	O	+	O
Cytoskeleton	O	O	+	O
Endoplasmic reticulum	O	O	+	O
Golgi apparatus	O	O	+	O
Lysosomes	O	+	O	O
Mitochondrion	O	O	+	O
Neurons	O	O	O	+
Nucleus	O	O	+	O
Peroxisomes	O	O	+	O
Ribosomes	O	O	+	O
Vacuoles	O	O	+	O

Figure 4.6 *Semantic feature analysis for cell parts*

ways for figuring out how these words work. They use the technical terms with one another and figure out the task at hand. They also trust one another and engage in interesting discussions about the ideas of biology. Mr. Bonine knows that his students will come to understand the academic vocabulary as they use it. He listens in on group conversations so he knows which words are still difficult for his students. With this information in mind, Mr. Bonine can plan subsequent opportunities for interaction as well as individual activities for his students.

Concept Circles: Understanding Attributes

To know a word is to know its attributes. Recall the contentious debate in 2006 among members of the International Astronomical Union as they argued, and eventually voted on, a definition of *planet*. We'd like to think that these experts would have agreed long ago about what constitutes a planet, but it turns out that the more you know about something, the more precise the language must be to describe and define it. After all, if it is round, large, and orbits a star, isn't it a planet? It turns out that this definition is simplistic, because it allows for too many objects to be classified as a planet. The experts determined that in order for something to be considered a planet, it also had to possess enough gravity to be able to clear a path for itself in its orbit; in other words, it had to be able to push other debris out of its way through gravity, not just collision.

If we arranged the pre- and post-August 2006 definitions of a planet into concept circles, they would look like Figure 4.7.

Poor little Pluto lost its status as a planet because of this change in definition. There is still much debate about this definition (particularly because Neptune doesn't completely sweep its orbit; Pluto is in the way), but the point here is that knowing the attributes of a word allows us to know the word. Concept circles are a way of representing those attributes visually through knowledge mapping.

Concept circles can be used in a variety of ways. The most obvious are ones that are teacher created, which are necessary for modeling how concept circles are developed and interpreted. Once students are comfortable with the process, allow them to create concept circles in partners or small groups. These student-created concept circles can be collected by the teacher and redistributed to other groups and used as games. Choose one of the following conditions for students to apply as they develop original concept circles:

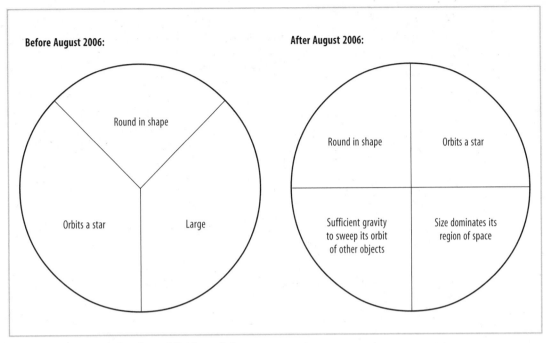

Figure 4.7 *Concept circles of two definitions of* planet

- Player identifies concepts based on attributes.

- Player identifies the incorrect attribute in a concept circle.

Danny and Steve developed a concept circle about free verse in their English class (see Figure 4.8). They were asked to use an incorrect attribute, so the boys decided to link some poets to this form. There had been confusion in the class regarding blank verse and free verse, so they identified a poet known for each of those types of poetic forms. Given their focus on attributes, concept circles are a great way for students to develop their outside-the-word problem-solving skills.

Shades of Meaning: Noticing Subtle Differences

The subtle differences between related words can be very confusing for students. While they might have a general sense of the difference between *overjoyed* and *ecstatic*, most students would be hard-pressed to define and use these terms in specific ways. In other words, most likely they would see these two

One of these attributes does not belong in a definition of free verse. Can you identify it correctly?

No regular rhyming pattern

Repeated sentence pattern

Used by Walt Whitman

Used by Shakespeare

Answer: Shakespeare did not write in free verse, but he did at times use blank verse.

Figure 4.8 *Concept circle for free verse in poetry*

words as synonyms and not comprehend the differences authors intend when they use one or the other.

Goodman (2004) developed the shades-of-meaning strategy as a way to address this need and help students develop their understanding that many words can be organized in gradients of meaning. The strategy encourages students to talk about words and arrange them along a continuum. As an interesting side note, the ability to distinguish subtle meaning is one of the skills assessed on the Scholastic Aptitude Test.

The easiest way to develop students' understanding of the differences between related words is to use paint chips. Most hardware stores will provide you with paint chips for free. Using a paint chip, students identify a continuum of words and then write the words in the colored sections of the paint chip.

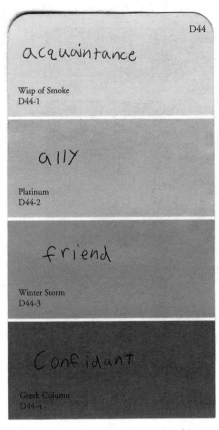

Figure 4.9 is a sample of a paint chip continuum related to friendship. The chip contains the following handwritten labels from light to dark:

- acquaintance — Wisp of Smoke D44-1
- ally — Platinum D44-2
- friend — Winter Storm D44-3
- Confidant — Greek Column D44-4

(D44)

Figure 4.9 *Shades-of-meaning paint chip*

Figure 4.9 contains a sample of a paint chip continuum related to friendship that a group of middle school students created after reading the book *Owen and Mzee: The True Story of a Remarkable Friendship* (Hatkoff, Hatkoff, and Kahumbu 2006).

As you can imagine, the conversations this group of students had about friendship and the words related to friendship was powerful. During their discussion, students used specialized words to convey their understandings. They also clarified their understanding of the words and provided one another with examples from their own experiences. For instance, Mubarik said, "*Ally* means friend, right? Someone who can help you, like provide assistance, like a friend."

Tynesia agreed but added, "I see a friend as an ally, but I think that an ally doesn't have the depth of a friendship. Friends are there regardless, in any circumstance. Being friends extends beyond being an ally."

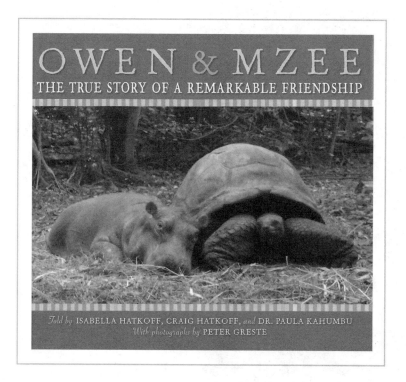

■ Written Approaches to Building Academic Vocabulary

The overarching goal of the interactive activities described in this section is to cause students to integrate Tier 2 and Tier 3 vocabulary into their written communication. The tasks involve traditional composition, and we know that the likelihood that students will use this vocabulary in written work increases as they have more opportunities to use academic vocabulary in their writing. As with the other strategies we've discussed, it is critical to select specific academic vocabulary for use with these activities. Middle and high school students simply do not have time to work with words they already know and use. They need to spend time integrating new technical vocabulary and novel uses of specialized vocabulary into their daily writing tasks.

Text Impressions: Making an Impact

Text impressions, also known as story impressions (McGinley and Denner 1987) and semantic impressions (Richek 2005), provide students an opportunity to build their academic vocabulary as they read a list of words, write a

Students using vocabulary while writing in history

paragraph containing those words, and then discuss the topic with their peers. The key to text impressions is the writing that students do. They have to place the words in context, often demonstrating their knowledge of the definitions, to write the paragraph.

The process for using text impressions is fairly simple. It starts with the teacher identifying key vocabulary words from an upcoming reading or unit of study. The selected words should meet the criteria outlined in Chapter 2, and the list of words should number between ten and twenty. Text impressions are most effective when there is a mix of specialized and technical words. Of course, students will not develop deep knowledge of all of these words from this one activity, but remember that this will not be the only exposure students have to the words. They'll read them or use them later.

Once the words have been selected, the teacher arranges the words and phrases vertically with arrows signifying the sequence in which they appear in the text. For example, Figure 4.10 contains a list of words used in a text impression in an earth science class. Students in the class were studying the Arctic region and were about to read a piece of text focused on the Arctic chill (Farndon 2007).

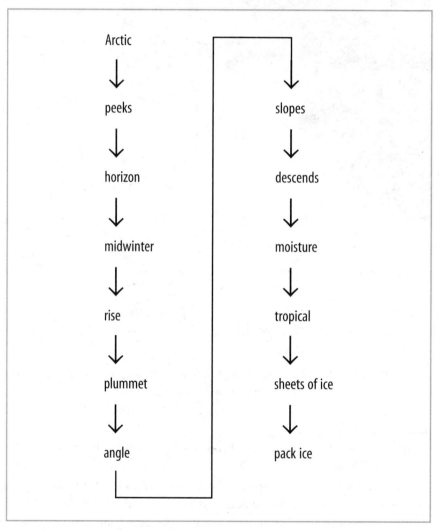

Figure 4.10 *Words selected for text impression*

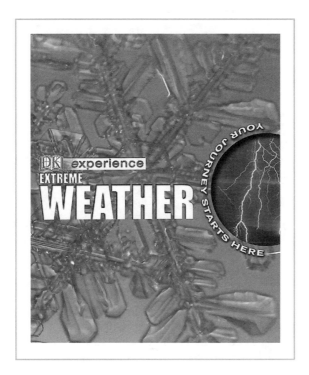

The teacher then introduces the words and phrases, explaining each. Typically, the teacher facilitates a conversation about the words and provides students opportunities to talk about the terms and ask questions. This generates a great deal of attention to the words. As the conversation comes to an end, students write paragraphs containing the words. Our experience suggests that these paragraphs are best written in partners or small groups. Of course, all of the students don't need to be working on this task at the same time, but they do need to accomplish it at some point in the lesson. Figure 4.11 contains the paragraph written by one of the groups in Ms. Harvey's class. Ms. Harvey has groups of students rotate through stations, completing different tasks during the period.

It's easy to see that the students in this group have a reasonable understanding of many of the academic vocabulary words, both specialized and technical, that they need to know to read the text. It's also easy to see that their understanding of some of the concepts is limited. For example, they may or may not know what *peeks* means. Similarly, the use of *horizon* is fairly basic and their understanding of the word will likely expand when they read the text and learn specific scientific information about horizons.

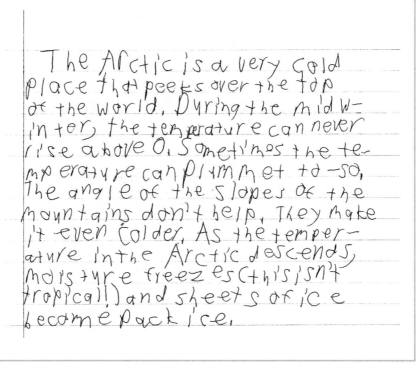

Figure 4.11 *Sample text impression paragraph*

When they have all completed their paragraphs, Ms. Harvey has her students share them with the class and discuss their thinking. After this has occurred, students can read the targeted text, looking for the words from the text impression chart. Ms. Harvey asks students to write definitions inferred from the reading on sticky notes when they find the words so that they can review their group paragraph and write an individual paragraph with more precise meanings for the selected words.

Text impressions provide students multiple opportunities to build their academic vocabulary. They can use both inside-the-word and outside-the-word strategies to think about word meaning. Inside-the-word strategies are fairly obvious; outside-the-word strategies may not be as obvious. To figure out unknown words, students will have to use other words on the list, information presented by the teacher, and data from the class discussion. As such, students build their academic vocabulary as they listen to their teacher introduce the words, when they talk about the words, as they write in small groups using the words, when they read a text containing the words, and finally as they write their own paragraph with enhanced knowledge of the words.

Collaborative Posters: A Meeting of the Minds

When students gather to work in groups of four or five, it can become more difficult for them to see their ideas and those of their partners represented on a document. We've been unsatisfied with allowing groups to select a recorder, because it generally devolves into the work of that one person. Instead, we ask them to work together on a collaborative poster. The written portion of the task is completed on chart paper, and each member has a marker in a different color. They sign the poster, making it easy for the teacher to identify the work of each student.

Rachelle, Amie, Lorena, and Brock created a collaborative poster in their English class using the book *The Outsiders* (Hinton 1995). They had selected this title from a list of thematically linked books on coming of age in America. Their task was to analyze the socioeconomic differences between two groups, the Socs and the Greasers, then link them to symbolic devices. After dividing the chart into three sections and labeling each column, the conversation began.

Rachelle: I think the obvious one is possessions. The Socs were rich and the Greasers didn't have anything.

Brock: Yeah, but we gotta go deeper. Like looking for the symbols of that.

Lorena: Cars. That's one.

Rachelle: Like what?

Lorena: Well, cars were the most important thing for the Socs . . .

Amie: Status symbol. No difference from now.

Lorena: Exactly. They all had these cars . . .

Brock: Not just cars. Expensive cars.

Brock: But the Greasers just fixed 'em. They were the repairmen.

Rachelle: Better put that down, both of you. Any other ideas?

The group continued its discussion of class symbolism for the next ten minutes and ended up with the poster shown in Figure 4.12.

Socs	Greasers	Symbolism
owned expensive cars	repaired cars	*status symbol*
short, conservative hairstyles	*long, greasy hair*	measure of conformity to society
Bob uses his rings in fights to hurt opponents	Two-Bit's switchblade	weapons connote strength and power

Lorena
Amie
Brock
Rachelle

Figure 4.12 *Collaborative poster for* The Outsiders

Vocabulary Games: Playing with Words

We opened this chapter with an example of the use of vocabulary games. We did so because we wanted to emphasize that academic vocabulary development can be fun. We also know that the use of vocabulary in games can be an effective way to build students' word knowledge (Beck, McKeown, and Kucan 2002; Richek 2005). For example, Selvidge (2006) demonstrated improved content knowledge as well as academic vocabulary development through the use of a board game focused on Egypt. In a study of college engineering students, Yip and Kwan (2006) demonstrated the positive impact that online vocabulary games had on student achievement.

From our experience, the key to using vocabulary games in the classroom lies in getting students to do the work—and getting each student to do a sufficient amount of work. When students write questions, for example, they have to consider the role that word meaning plays in the answers. Similarly, as they construct games, students have to consider the multiple meanings of words so that they don't confuse their players. There are a number of vocabulary games that teachers can use to build students' academic vocabulary, including

● *Crossword Puzzles*: Student-created crossword puzzles require that students focus on word meanings, providing just enough information but not too much information. Discovery Education offers a web-based puzzle-creation tool that students can use to create their masterpieces (http://puzzlemaker.school.discovery.com).

- *Jeopardy! Wheel of Fortune,* and *Who Wants to Be a Millionaire?* Following the formats of popular TV quiz shows, students create questions and answers based on specific vocabulary words. Again, the goal is to provide increasingly difficult questions to elicit responses. There are free PowerPoint downloads students can use to create these games at http://jc-schools.net/tutorials/vocab/ppt-vocab.html.

- *Wordo*: Students enter vocabulary words into the squares of a bingo card and then write definitions for each of the terms. The teacher can call definitions while students mark off the words. Again, the key is to have students develop the game. A sample Wordo card can be found in Figure 4.13.

- *Flip-a-Chip*: Lee Mountain (2002) developed this game that uses poker chips or any other small round chips. After being introduced to the game, students write prefixes, suffixes, and bases on the chips. They then flip the chips and determine if the resulting word is real or not. Mountain introduces the game with two chips. On the first, one side says *pro-* and the other says *re-*. On the second chip, one side says *-duce* and the other says *-voke*. By flipping the two chips, students see that they can make the following words: *produce, provoke, reduce,* and *revoke*. By adding affixes and roots themselves, students learn a variety of combinations that do and do not produce real words.

Of course there are many other vocabulary games that students can play that build their academic vocabulary. As you can see, each of these games involves students writing and using the words. They are also talking with one another and creating visuals. In doing so, they are building their stores of words and beginning to use these words as they complete tasks, engage with others, and read increasingly complex texts.

■ Conclusion

Vocabulary learners need time to build their understanding of words and terms through peer interactions. Regular use of partner and small-group discussion provides students with opportunities to clarify their thinking and extend each other's knowledge. Other interactions that utilize oral language include jigsaws, which encourage learners to retell new information, and reciprocal teaching, which formalizes the comprehension strategies used by proficient readers. Student think-alouds extend the work of the teacher, as described in Chapter 3, by shifting the cognitive load to the learner as she builds metacognition.

Other strategies capitalize on the visual arrangement of information in order for students to create knowledge maps that show relationships between and

WORDO

		Free Space!		

Figure 4.13 *Sample Wordo card*

among words. Word mapping allows students to arrange information in a hierarchical manner, from larger concepts to smaller details. Semantic feature analysis adds another level of complexity, as students juxtapose ideas across two planes in a matrix form. Concept circles allow students to consider the attributes of a word, while the shades-of-meaning strategy encourages students to see a group of related words on a continuum or gradient of intensity.

The final group of peer interaction activities ask learners to apply their growing word knowledge using writing. Working together, they analyze a list of words and link them into a paragraph that might predict the reading to come. Collaborative posters move small-group work from the task of one recorder to a shared responsibility where all members are required to contribute their ideas in writing. Lastly, students play and create original games for others utilizing the vocabulary of the content. These playful development tasks extend student learning beyond passive experiences. Building vocabulary requires active learning, and peer interactions let students see words from the inside and the outside, making academic vocabulary a part of *their* everyday discourse. Thus, the acquisition of words and ideas becomes central to their lives rather than something school focused, and we all get that much closer to achieving true content knowledge.

5

Make It Personal
Consolidating Students' Academic Vocabulary Through Individual Activities

Bao empties the contents of the envelope given to him by his prealgebra teacher. Sixteen small slips of paper spill out onto his desktop.

"Good morning, everyone," announces Ms. Reiss. "I want you to sort the math terms you see into any categories you wish. Move them around until you're satisfied. When you're ready, glue them onto a paper and write the names of the categories you've chosen. There's no one correct way of doing it. I'm interested in seeing how you think. I'm still getting to know all of you as mathematicians, and this activity is going to help me a lot." Ms. Reiss does this open sorting activity every year during the first week of school. While the students dive into the task, Ms. Reiss walks around the room, watching how they approach the task.

Bao recognizes some of the terms, but others are unfamiliar. He moves them around on his desk, exchanging terms between categories several times. His finished sort is shown in Figure 5.1.

Ms. Reiss meets with each student in the days that follow to find out more about their reasoning. When she sits with Bao, she asks him to explain his categories. "I moved them around in lots of ways. I figured that some of these were stuff I already learned, like all the operations. There were some words I knew had to do with algebra, because my sister took it last year and we do our homework in the same room. I figured you're gonna teach us that stuff this year. I made the next category as fractions, but that might not be right.

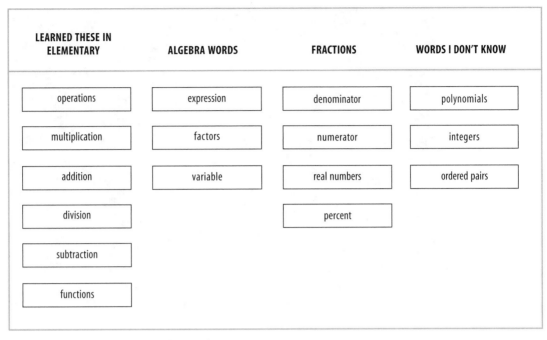

LEARNED THESE IN ELEMENTARY	ALGEBRA WORDS	FRACTIONS	WORDS I DON'T KNOW
operations	expression	denominator	polynomials
multiplication	factors	numerator	integers
addition	variable	real numbers	ordered pairs
division		percent	
subtraction			
functions			

Figure 5.1 *Bao's open sort of mathematical terms*

Like, I know percents and fractions are kinda the same, but I don't know. Then there was stuff I never heard of before ever, so I just made a pile called 'Words I Don't Know.'"

In a few minutes, Ms. Reiss has learned quite a bit about Bao's mathematical knowledge and the way he organizes his understandings. She has made notes as he's talked, and these will help her teach to his needs. In turn, Bao has also learned some things about what he knows, and does not know so well, and he's had a chance to meet one-on-one with Ms. Reiss, which makes him feel good about math class. The individual time has been valuable to both of them.

■ The Power of Individual Learning

It may sound melodramatic, but spending just three minutes talking with a student about his work can be transformative for both the teacher and the learner. When we take the time to meet individually with students and invite them to articulate their reasoning about their independent work, it helps them consolidate their thinking and helps us identify strengths and needs with maximum efficiency. Why, then, has independent learning gotten such a bad

Students word sorting

reputation over the years? In a word, *worksheets*. When you hear "independent work," the first image that comes to mind is of students doing lots of fairly superficial worksheets in and out of school. We're not fans of endless streams of worksheets, either, and we are quite concerned at the amount of time students spend working independently. A large-scale study of 737 fifth-grade classrooms in 33 states found that students spent 38 percent of their time doing individual seatwork (Pianta et al. 2007). Our intuition and our experiences tell us that this percentage is even higher in middle and high school.

As a profession, we've got to stop equating independent learning with busy-work and instead give it the exulted place it deserves. We want to make a case for independent work becoming a vital part of content area learning in general and vocabulary learning in particular. Think about it: without it, all our teaching disappears like wisps of smoke. It's in an individual student's solo work that we see she has *learned*—she has *applied* what we've taught her. Independent work is the final phase of the gradual release of responsibility model of instruction, capping off the modeling and guided practice phases. Race (1996) argues that all learning is ultimately independent, in the sense that it doesn't really become known until it becomes a part of the individual's knowledge base; collective knowledge alone won't cut it. Our goal as teachers is for students to become independent learners, especially as they near adulthood and will need to sustain their own learning outside of the academic environment. This is where we think independent learning breaks down in too many classrooms: Independent *for* whom and independent *from* whom? We need to consider whether the activity is contributing to their knowledge of themselves as learners or if it is merely an activity that keeps them independent from *us*.

What does an independent learner look like? Before we develop activities that we think will foster independence and further students' understandings, we've found it helpful to sketch a profile of such learners' features. Murdoch and Wilson (2006) analyzed the research on effective independent learners and synthesized the findings into three main characteristics:

- *Independent learners are self-motivators*. These students can establish goals and monitor their progress toward them; they are willing to take risks; and they welcome challenge.

- *Independent learners are self-managers*. They try to solve their own problems, manage their time, and think creatively.

- *Independent learners are self-appraisers.* They accurately assess what they know and don't know; they notice their own learning; and they act upon their learning by applying strategies they know to be useful for learning.

As you plan independent vocabulary activities, measure them against these qualities as a way to check their effectiveness. Ask yourself: *Does this activity significantly contribute to my students' development as self-motivated, self-managed, and self-appraising learners?* If we can be honest with ourselves about our independent learning practices, we will be in good stead.

■ Characteristics of Effective Individual Learning

In our discussion of independent learning, which should be a key component of the instructional design of a class, we must not forget the individual learner. The room may be bulging at the seams with thirty-five or more learners, but each is unique in terms of background knowledge, habits of mind, and interests. There isn't any practical way to teach each student individually, and even if there were, we wouldn't advocate for it anyway. But even in a crowd, we have to set the conditions for individual learning with the same care that we apply to independent learning. The conditions for successful individual learning include:

- *Choice*: Adolescents need options in how they can approach a task. That's why worksheets and end-of-chapter questions are so demoralizing. Activities that result in unique responses are more engaging.

- *Differentiation*: This doesn't mean thirty-five different assignments, but it does mean that the tasks can vary depending on the needs and proclivities of the student. This is especially true with academic vocabulary development. Students don't arrive at our classroom door in possession of the same bank of words at their disposal. The vocabulary they are responsible for at the individual level should differ so that it aligns more closely with what they currently need to learn.

- *Relevance*: If it feels like busywork, it is doomed to fail. Teachers have to make sure students see how the individual activities relate to the unit of study. In addition, teachers should be explicit about the ways in which they are helping students develop into self-regulated learners. Adolescents are eager to show that they are not children anymore. Use their desire for the trappings of adulthood by encouraging their independence as learners— perhaps the most important adult behavior of all.

■ Moving from Building to Consolidating

In the last chapter, we spoke of the need for students to build their knowledge of words through peer interactions. These collaborative experiences encourage learners to use specialized and technical vocabulary in their oral language, to negotiate meaning through joint development of knowledge maps, and to apply terminology during group writing. These building experiences must be followed by well-crafted individual activities that allow students to consolidate their understanding of the definitional, contextual, and conceptual knowledge of words.

Nagy (1988) reminds us that three conditions are needed for a student to learn vocabulary: integration, repetition, and meaningful use. Individual learning experiences provide students with these opportunities in the following ways:

- *integration* with schemata through a focus on "sets of relationships," not isolated facts (10);

- *repetition* through multiple opportunities to encounter a new word in speech, reading, and writing; and

- *meaningful use* that "makes students think about the meaning of the word and demands they do some . . . processing of the word" (24).

The individual learning activities in this chapter were selected based on their properties of integration, repetition, and meaningful use. In addition, we looked for activities that could meet the needs of individual learners regarding choice, differentiation, and relevance. Finally, we analyzed each to determine whether the activity fostered development as self-motivators, self-managers, and self-appraisers. We have grouped these activities into three categories. The first group of activities asks students to log their knowledge in ways that cause them

Student studying word cards in English

to consider what they know and don't know. The second category invites students to mentally and physically manipulate words using sorts, word cards, and mnemonic devices. The final type encourages them to compose using the targeted academic vocabulary.

■ Consolidating Individual Learning Through Logs

The ability to know what one knows, as well as what is not known, is a key aspect to metacognitive awareness. The goal of this process isn't merely to catalog one's knowledge, but to set goals, a fundamental characteristic of self-regulated learners (Ridley et al. 1992). The following three activities encourage individual learners to notice their learning and witness their progress toward learning goals.

Vocabulary Self-Awareness: Self-Monitoring in Action

One of the reasons that academic vocabulary instruction has been so difficult to change revolves around the fact that students differ in their baseline understanding of words. Take, for example, a typical class of ninth-grade students. The group's differences in vocabulary knowledge are likely to range by about eight years. Some students will have word knowledge profiles of students in third or fourth grade while others will possess extensive vocabularies that earn them post–high school scores on vocabulary assessments.

Understanding that there are differences in individual vocabulary attainment is the primary reason why this system works. We know that students benefit from modeling and using words with their peers. But if academic vocabulary instruction ended there, students would not attain high levels of literacy achievement. As teachers, we simply must provide opportunities for students to consolidate their academic vocabulary development.

One of the ways we do this is through vocabulary self-assessments (e.g., Goodwin 2001). As a target word is encountered, students can add it to their self-awareness charts and determine if they know the word, have just heard the word, or if the word is new to them. While some words, especially technical words, are provided to everyone in the class, other words are provided to specific students. As such, each student might have different words on his vocabulary self-awareness chart. Both teachers and students can determine which words to add to their charts. We know that self-selection of vocabulary enhances students' motivation and achievement in learning new words (Ruddell and Shearer 2002). In addition, when students can explain their rationale for adding words to their charts, they develop their metacognitive skills and word consciousness. Even further, as they incorporate definitions and examples into their knowledge bases, they consolidate their knowledge of inside- and outside-the-word solving strategies.

Figure 5.2 contains a modified vocabulary self-assessment chart. Students enter a date for the level of knowledge they have when they first encounter the word. As they become more comfortable with the word, they add dates in advancing levels. As you can see in this figure, Tino's class was focused on matter and motion. As he incorporated specific terms into his knowledge base, he updated the chart. Not all of the words on Tino's chart could be found on

Word	Level A	Level B	Level C	Example	Definition
Motion		10/1	10/15	The car was in motion when the driver attempted to stop.	When an object changes position over time in relation to a reference point.
Speed			10/1	The driver was speeding when she was pulled over by the cops.	How fast an object moves. Add rate -- it's the rate of how fast the object moves.
Force	10/1	10/15	10/21	The force of the car's impact crushed the tree.	A push or pull.
Friction		10/1	10/21	Friction helps the car's breaks lower the speed of the car in motion.	Force that opposes motion between two surfaces that are touching.

Level A = a word that is new to me
Level B = a word I have heard and can either define or give an example of, but not both
Level C = a word I'm familiar with and can both define and provide an example

Figure 5.2 *Vocabulary self-awareness chart*

the charts of his peers. These are the words that Tino and his teacher thought were important for him to learn.

A–Z Charts: Topical Word Lists

A–Z charts are another way that individuals can track what they know and what they learn, in terms of academic vocabulary, during a unit of study. These simple charts, like the one in Figure 5.3, contain alphabetically arranged blocks for students to record the words they know based on the given topic. There are a number of ways to use the A–Z chart (Allen 2000). We prefer to ask students to identify words and phrases they know about the topic and log them on the chart as an anticipatory activity, before any instruction. Then, as the unit progresses, individual students add various words to their charts.

As part of his unit on adaptation, Mr. Close distributed blank copies of an A–Z chart to his students. He asked them to identify words and phrases that they knew related to adaptation. Given that this was the first time he had used an A–Z chart, students were unsure what to do. Tami said, "We don't know anything about this yet and you're already giving us a test?" Mr. Close assured his students that this was not a test, but rather an opportunity to identify what they already knew so that he could focus his instruction on what each student needed to learn. The students started working, listing words and phrases that they associated with adaptation.

As they finished this opening exercise, Mr. Close asked his students to draw a line in each box under the last word or phrase entered. Over the course of two weeks, as students engaged in the unit of study, Mr. Close reminded them to update their A–Z charts. They added information from lectures, readings, films, and labs to their charts. Tami's chart, with a line drawn under the words that she knew at the outset of the unit, can be found in Figure 5.4. Note how many more words she knew by the end of the unit. There are some boxes with no lines because she did not have any words to include during the opening activity.

Importantly, A–Z charts also help teachers identify words that students believe they know. This information can be used as a formative assessment in that the teacher may notice that some students don't seem to know a lot of words related to the content being studied and may, thus, need additional instruction. The teacher may also notice that some students are not adding to their A–Z charts and wonder if this group of students is failing to focus on academic vocabulary. In addition, teachers can use A–Z charts as a source of checking vocabulary knowledge. By sitting with a student and looking at his chart,

A–B	C–D	E–F
G–H	I–J	K–L
M–N	O–P–Q	R–S
T–U	V–W–X	Y–Z

Figure 5.3 *A–Z chart*

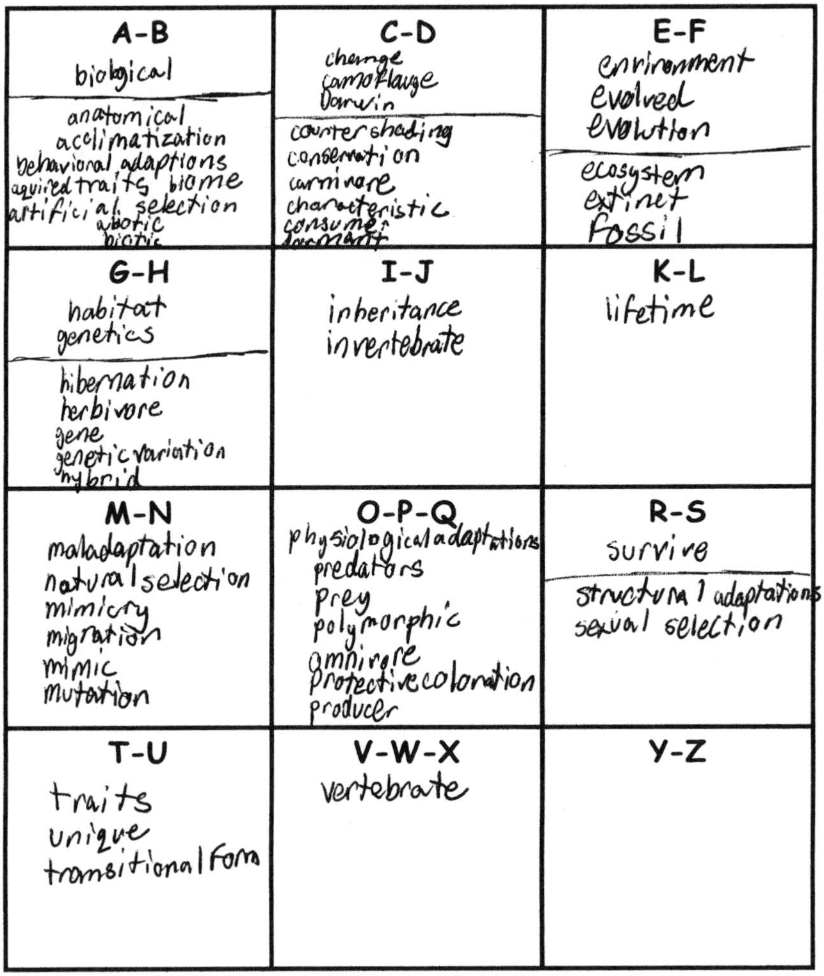

A–B	C–D	E–F
biological	change camoflauge Darwin	environment evolved evolution
anatomical acclimatization behavioral adaptions acquired traits biome artificial selection abiotic biotic	counter shading conservation carnivore characteristic consumer dormant	ecosystem extinct fossil
G–H	**I–J**	**K–L**
habitat genetics	inheritance invertebrate	lifetime
hibernation herbivore gene genetic variation hybrid		
M–N	**O–P–Q**	**R–S**
maladaptation natural selection mimicry migration mimic mutation	physiological adaptations predators prey polymorphic omnivore protective coloration producer	survive structural adaptations sexual selection
T–U	**V–W–X**	**Y–Z**
traits unique transitional form	vertebrate	

FIGURE 5.4 *Tami's A–Z chart on adaptation*

the teacher can discuss word meanings and see if the student really has a grasp of the words listed on the chart.

Vocabulary Journals: Keeping Track of Words

As we have discussed, students learn and retain academic vocabulary in a variety of ways. Of course, students need opportunities to interact with the words, especially in peer contexts. However, students also need a place to keep track of the words they're learning. An effective way to accomplish this is through a vocabulary journal (Fisher and Frey 2008). With vocabulary journals, students clarify unfamiliar words or phrases by listing them on a chart in their journals. They can identify words themselves, or their teachers can identify words to be added to journals.

Vocabulary journal entries can have all kinds of components. Our colleague Constantina Burow requires that students create interactive vocabulary journals in their geometry classes. As can be seen in the student sample in Figure 5.5, Ms. Burow is interested in her students' understanding of key terms, formulas,

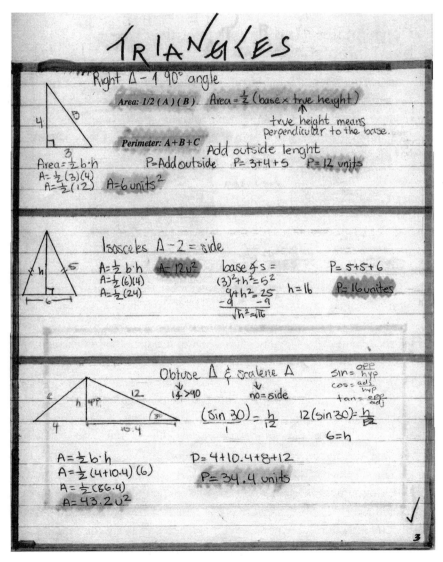

Figure 5.5 *Geometry vocabulary journal*

diagrams, and theorems related to those terms, evidence of the terms in real life, and summaries of the terms.

Of course, there are no hard-and-fast rules about what to include in a vocabulary journal. In our own teaching, we focus students on specialized vocabulary words. As can be seen in the vocabulary journal in Figure 5.6, students were asked to collect words that had meanings different from what they thought. This journal also required that students think about how they figured out the word—from context clues, word parts, or resources.

■ Consolidating Individual Learning by Manipulating Words

The physical and mental manipulation of words is an extension of the visual methods outlined in the previous chapter. These techniques cause learners to consolidate definitional, contextual, and conceptual understandings of words by engaging in sorting activities, creating word cards for studying, and developing mnemonic devices for promoting recall and retrieval.

Word Sorts: Organizing Word Knowledge

Sorting words causes students to consider the relationships between and among groups of words. At its simplest level, a student groups related words into categories by considering the attributes or properties represented by each word. The example at the beginning of this chapter illustrated how Bao sorted mathematical terms and explained his thinking to his teacher.

There are three basic kinds of word sorts: closed, open, and conceptual. Closed sorts come with categories furnished in advance by the teacher, while open sorts require the student to develop original categories (Bear et al. 2007). While word sorts for young learners involve phonics and spelling patterns, the ones we use with middle and high school students are conceptual. These sorts should be performed using words printed on individual slips of paper. While this may seem burdensome to prepare, the usefulness of a sorting activity is in providing the maximum amount of flexibility to the learner as she contemplates possible categorical arrangements. We have tried to take the easy way out by giving students a list of words to write in their own categories and have discovered that they are far less likely to experiment this way. They dislike erasing anything once they've written it and will sort using the most obvious categories possible. In order to reduce the teacher preparation time, ask students to cut their own word slips and write the assigned words on them. They

WORD	WHAT I THINK IT MEANS	WHAT IT ACTUALLY MEANS	CLUES (context or parts)	WHERE I FOUND OUT

Figure 5.6 *Vocabulary journal*

can then glue the words onto a notebook page and write an explanation of their thinking.

Since you have already read about the way an open conceptual word sort might be used in a classroom, we'll show you how one of Bao's classmates sorted her words (see Figure 5.7).

Michelle saw a different organization in the words in front of her. In particular, she perceived that many of these terms represented mathematical functions. For example, she broke apart the basic terms of operation and described them as ways in which numbers are increased and reduced. Importantly, she recognized that *integer*, *factors*, *real numbers*, and *percent* could describe different ways in which numbers could be represented. "When I spoke to Michelle about her word sort, I realized that this was a student who was moving beyond algorithms and is really thinking about the purposes for doing math," said Ms. Reiss. "She's already displaying that abstract reasoning that other students don't have. This tells me that she is ready to be challenged even further."

REDUCING	INCREASING	DESCRIBING NUMBERS	FINDING SOLUTIONS
denominator	addition	integers	polynomials
division	multiplication	factors	variable
subtraction		real numbers	expression
numerator		percent	operations

NUMBER RELATIONSHIPS

subtraction

functions

Figure 5.7 *Michelle's open sort of mathematics terms*

Word Cards: Consolidating Through Repeated Practice

Word cards are a powerful way for students to think about words, especially because they can be used to help students consolidate their understanding of academic vocabulary terms. Of course, word selection is critical. Students should be spending time focused on words that they need to know, which have been either self-selected or suggested by their teacher.

One of the ways that students consolidate their understanding of academic vocabulary terms is to focus for more than a few seconds on the words. That's one of the reasons that word cards are effective; they take a little time and effort to complete. In addition, word cards provide students an opportunity to review key terms. That's the other reason they're effective: learners need multiple opportunities to interact with words before they know them.

Our vocabulary cards are based on the Frayer model (e.g., Frayer, Frederick, and Klausmeier 1969) and encourage learners to think about new vocabulary through definition, contrasts, and visual representations (see Figure 5.8). They are typically developed using a five-by-seven-inch index card divided into four quadrants. Naturally, there are a number of variations of word cards. Some teachers like sentences written on the cards; others do not. Some teachers focus on synonyms and antonyms, while others do not. We prefer to have students illustrate the term on the word card (in one of the quadrants on the back), as this requires that they think about the word using a different part of their brain.

An updated version of vocabulary cards, *vocabutoons*, was developed by a high school student studying for his SAT exams. In his own words:

> As a high school student in 1980, preparing for the verbal section of the SAT was dull and laborious. Each night after dinner my dad would work with me on improving my vocabulary skills. I dreaded it, until one night I had trouble remembering the definition to the word "aloof." My dad asked me "What rhymes with aloof?" I said, "Roof." So, my dad replied, "Okay, think of the cat on the roof is aloof from everyone below." Voila! That little mnemonic mental image was permanently imbedded in my brain. After that it was actually fun coming up with crazy ways to remember meanings of words. (www.vocabularycartoons.com/aboutaus.aspx)

Based on his experience, Bryan and his brother and father published a series of books using cartoons and word cards to teach academic vocabulary. For example, their version of the word *lament* is shown in Figure 5.9. We like vocabutoons and use these books in our classrooms. We also encourage

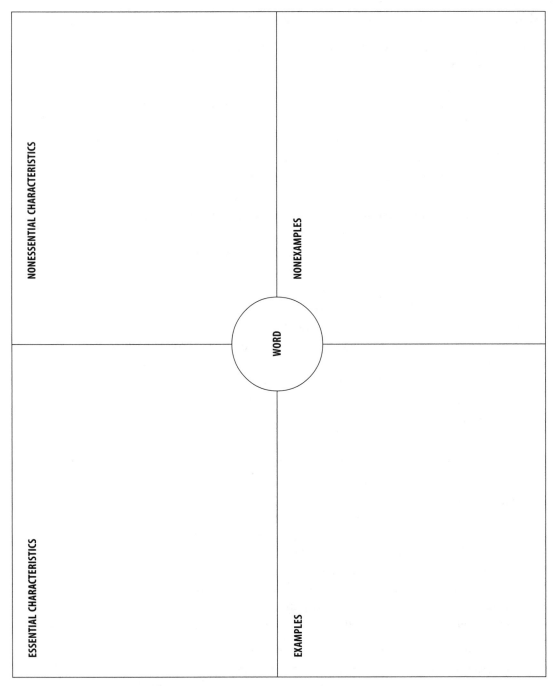

Figure 5.8 *Vocabulary card based on Frayer model*

students to create their own vocabutoons to help them consolidate their understanding of the words.

Mnemonics: Memory Builders

Keyword mnemonics were first used to teach students studying a foreign language (Raugh and Atkinson 1975) and soon became popular for teaching vocabulary for any learner (Pressley, Levin, and Delaney 1983). The word *mnemonics*

LAMENT
(luh MINT) *v.*
to express sorrow or regret; to mourn
Link: **CEMENT**

"We **LAMENT** that Joe got buried in **CEMENT**."

- The song, "Cowboy's **LAMENT**," is a ballad about the lonely life of those who drive cattle for a living.
- The nation **LAMENTS** the passing of the President while at the same time celebrating his achievements while in office.
- It is **LAMENTABLE** that Roscoe quit college in his sophomore year; his professors considered him the brightest engineering student in his class.

Figure 5.9 *Vocabutoon*

comes from the Greek word *mnemonikos*, meaning mindful. Mnemonic devices are used to recall information. For example, many of us have learned to use FOIL to remind ourselves of the steps for multiplying binomials—*first, outside, inside, last.* Doug memorized the lobes of the brain for his neuroanatomy class using FPOT: *frontal, parietal, occipital,* and *temporal.* This is called a *peg mnemonic* because each letter reminds one of an item on a list.

The keyword method of vocabulary attainment involves two other aspects of mnemonic devices: an acoustical element and a visual one. It is believed that memory is enhanced when two stimuli are closely associated with one another, known more formally as *dual coding theory* (Paivio 1969). You have already seen the usefulness of visual and acoustical mnemonics in vocabutoons. These techniques are widely used for memorization and recall of complex information in the fields of pathology, medicine, pharmacology, and aviation. For example, a mnemonic that uses dual coding involves Felty's syndrome, a complication that can arise because of rheumatoid arthritis. One of the markers of the disease is that the spleen can be *felt* (Felty's) upon examination. Many people who have passed national professional board examinations owe their thanks in part to mnemonics for recalling information.

Let's return to the word *mnemonics* to demonstrate the usefulness of keyword learning as it relates to roots and word derivation. We told you that it

Student creating mnemonics

stems from the Greek word for mindfulness. The word is also closely related to Mnemosyne, the mother of the Muses in mythology. Now add a visual to that—imagine a Greek goddess who *mindfully* watches over her daughters. She encourages them to *remember* where they came from, and to keep the *memory* of their family close to their hearts. That mental image of the mindful mother, along with the acoustically similar words *mindful*, *remember*, and *memory* consolidate a dual association in your mind. Chances are that if you invested your attention in that word, you will recall the word and its image long after you have closed this book.

Mnemonics are a useful way for individual learners to mentally manipulate sound and image to create a memory that can be retrieved on demand. We teach our students to use mnemonics as a way to independently learn information and vocabulary. In fact, the information we shared about Mnemosyne is how we introduce the technique to our students. We ask them to think of peg mnemonics they have already learned, and we usually hear about HOMES to recall the names of the Great Lakes (Huron, Ontario, Michigan, Erie, and Superior), or Please Excuse My Dear Aunt Sally to remind us of the order of operations in mathematics (parentheses, exponents, multiplication, division, addition, subtraction). We also give them opportunities to develop their own peg and keyword mnemonics, as the most valuable ones seem to be those that are created by the learner, rather than provided by the teacher. At the secondary level, students are often required to recall extensive amounts of information, so we remind them to incorporate this approach in their own independent learning.

For example, Cal had been studying for an upcoming Advanced Placement exam in U.S. history and needed to be able to recall some of the key battles of the Civil War. "I needed to remember the order, not so much because of the dates, but because each of these battles resulted in an important development for either the Union Army or the Confederacy," he explained. Cal had used mnemonics with some success in his other classes, so he decided to devise one for himself on the major battles. He first listed the names he wanted to remember:

Fort Sumter (1861)

Bull Run 1 (1861)

Shiloh (1862)

Bull Run 2 (1862)

Antietam (1862)

Gettysburg (1863)

Tupelo (1864)

Atlanta (1865)

Appomattox (1865)

He then listed the first letter of each battle: *F, B, S, B, A, G, T, A, A*. Not finding any obvious words in this group of letters, he began to create a sentence. In the course of a few minutes, he created one he found satisfactory: "French bread smells better after going to an arena." He sketched a cartoon drawing of a person holding his nose as he walked away from a sports arena. "I imaged what a smelly locker room in a sports arena would smell like, and how good a whiff of fresh-baked French bread would be." Of course, each of these battle names represents far more information than the label alone implies. But Cal's creation of a personal mnemonic allowed him to recall a sequence of information and access the schema he had developed for this content and words used to convey the information.

■ Consolidating Individual Learning Through Composing

In addition to logging words and physically and mentally manipulating words, students consolidate their understanding when they compose using academic vocabulary. Composing with scaffolds and supports compels learners to focus on word meanings and how words fit into sentences and paragraphs. It is important to note that asking students to write using targeted vocabulary comes later in the process of developing academic word knowledge. Students working at the individual learning level have had multiple exposures to words in order to develop some depth and breadth to their word knowledge.

Generative Sentences: Constructing from the Given

One of the ways students consolidate their knowledge of academic vocabulary is to use specific words in constructed sentences (Fisher and Frey 2007). Generative sentences involve students constructing sentences from words that are given to them. Fearn and Farnan call this practice a "given word sentence" (2001, 87). We have extended their ideas and focus on the generative nature of the composing process that requires students to move from the word, to the sentence, to the paragraph level.

This strategy allows students to expand their sentences and to be able to use the academic vocabulary and mechanics that are necessary in order to convey information. Essentially, the teacher identifies a letter or word and the place in a sentence where the word will be used. Students then write sentences with the given components. The key to generative sentences is to vary the placement of the word (e.g., first position, last position, some numbered position) and the length of the sentence (e.g., exactly x number of words, fewer than x number of words, or more than x number of words). These variations require that students consider the complexity of the word and how it can be used, correctly, in a sentence.

For example, in our study of a gradual release of responsibility model of writing instruction, we asked struggling adolescent readers to write the letter *v* on their paper (Fisher and Frey 2003). The next instruction was to write a word with the letter *v* in the third position. A list of words was then recorded on the dry-erase board. Students were able to see the variation of words that share this characteristic—*love, have, give, dove, advice,* and so on. Following this, we asked students to use their word in a sentence. Following are a few of the sentences:

- I love my family, especially James.

- The dove is a sign of peace.

- You best get some advice on that hairdo.

Once students are familiar with the task, the teacher can focus on specialized and academic vocabulary words. By requiring that specific words be used in specific places within sentences, teachers encourage students to use their knowledge of vocabulary and grammar to demonstrate their thinking. We recommend that students complete five generative sentences per class per day. This provides them practice with composing using specific academic vocabulary. Our experience suggests that the selected words should be a mix of specialized and technical terms. This individual activity provides the teacher with an opportunity to check for understanding. By reviewing students' generative sentences, the teacher can determine the depth of students' understanding and identify students who need additional assistance. This level of independent work with words is based on a great deal of instruction and is not simply asking students to define words.

Take, for example, the following sentences written by two different students. The sentences clearly demonstrate the two students' thinking about the word *avalanche*. The prompt required that students use the word *avalanche* in the third position.

- When the Avalanche play, the world of hockey pays attention.

- The worst avalanche in history occurred in Peru in 1970.

Both students used the term correctly, one for a sports team in Colorado and one for a natural disaster. While their teacher was focused on natural disasters, one of these students was not.

In a middle school science class focused on animal adaptation, the teacher used generative sentences on a daily basis. During the part of the unit on physical adaptation, the teacher shared the book *Animal Disguises* (Weber 2004). Given that the words in the book should have been familiar to her students, this science teacher asked her students to compose the following five sentences:

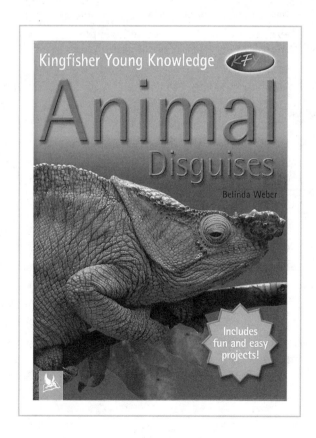

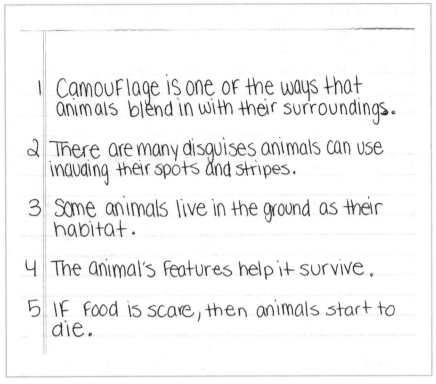

Figure 5.10 *Vanessa's generative sentences for* Animal Disguises

1. *camouflage* in the first position of a sentence of any length
2. *disguise(s)* in the fourth position of a sentence of more than eight words
3. *habitat* in the last position of a sentence of fewer than ten words
4. *features* in the third position of a sentence of any length
5. an *if . . . then* sentence about animal adaptation

It is clear from Vanessa's writing (see Figure 5.10) that she understood most of these words. Given her response to the prompt about *habitat*, and the lack of sophistication this response demonstrated, her teacher decided to focus some additional instructional time with her to focus on this concept.

Writing Frames: Providing Structure for Words

In our study of struggling adolescent writers (2003), we noted that the use of writing models such as sentence and paragraph frames provided students with scaffolds such that they could write more sophisticated compositions. These writing frames also helped students focus on the words they were learning by removing some of the task demands related to composition. We know that students write less-sophisticated sentences and paragraphs when they have not internalized academic writing.

College composition experts Gerald Graff and Cathy Birkenstein (2006) recommend the use of frames (they call them templates) as an effective way for developing students' academic writing skills. They suggest that students be systematically taught these frames because they are models of academic writing. They defend the use of frames or templates by suggesting

> After all, even the most creative forms of expression depend on established patterns and structures. Most songwriters, for instance, rely on a time-honored verse-chorus-verse pattern, and few people would call Shakespeare uncreative because he didn't invent the sonnet or dramatic forms that he used to such dazzling effect. . . . Ultimately, then, creativity and originality lie not in the avoidance of established forms, but in the imaginative use of them. (10–11)

As Graff and Birkenstein correctly note, writing frames help students incorporate established norms of academic writing into their repertoires. Writing frames provide students practice in the discourse patterns expected of educated citizens. In addition, based on our classroom experiences, we know writing frames provide students an opportunity to consolidate their understanding of specialized and technical terms as they use them to share their thinking.

At the most basic level, teachers can use frames around specific academic words to help students incorporate target words into their writing. Consider the use of writing frames related to persuasion. The students in Mr. Jackson's English class were focused on developing their persuasive writing skills. They did so by incorporating a number of frames into their habits (see Figure 5.11).

Importantly, writing frames are not limited to use in the English classroom. For instance, a biology teacher provided her students with a writing frame focused on DNA. She used a summary writing frame based on the work of Lewis and Wray (1995), which read:

> Although I already knew that _____, I have learned some new facts about _____. For example, I learned that _____. I also learned that _____. Another fact I learned _____. However the most interesting thing I learned was _____. (1995, 27)

With repeated practice with writing frames at both the sentence and the paragraph levels, students become increasingly proficient in their writing and

Making a claim

• My own view is that _____ , because _____ .

• Though I agree that _____ , I still maintain that _____ .

• She argues _____ , and I agree, because _____ .

Supporting/critiquing a claim

• Her argument that _____ is supported by _____ , _____ , and _____ .

• For example, _____ shows that _____ .

• Their assertion that _____ is contradicted by _____ , _____ , and _____ .

Introducing and addressing a counterargument

• Of course, some might disagree with my claim and say that _____ .

• Some might object that _____ , but I would reply that _____ .

• While it is true that _____ , that does not necessarily mean that _____ .

Stating a conclusion or summing up an argument

• In conclusion, I believe _____ .

• In sum: _____ is demonstrated by _____ and _____ .

• For these reasons, _____ should be _____ .

From *Word Wise and Content Rich, Grades 7–12*. Porstmouth, NH: Heinemann. © 2009 Clencoe Literature. Used with permission of Glencoe/McGraw-Hill.

Figure 5.11 *Persuasive writing frames*

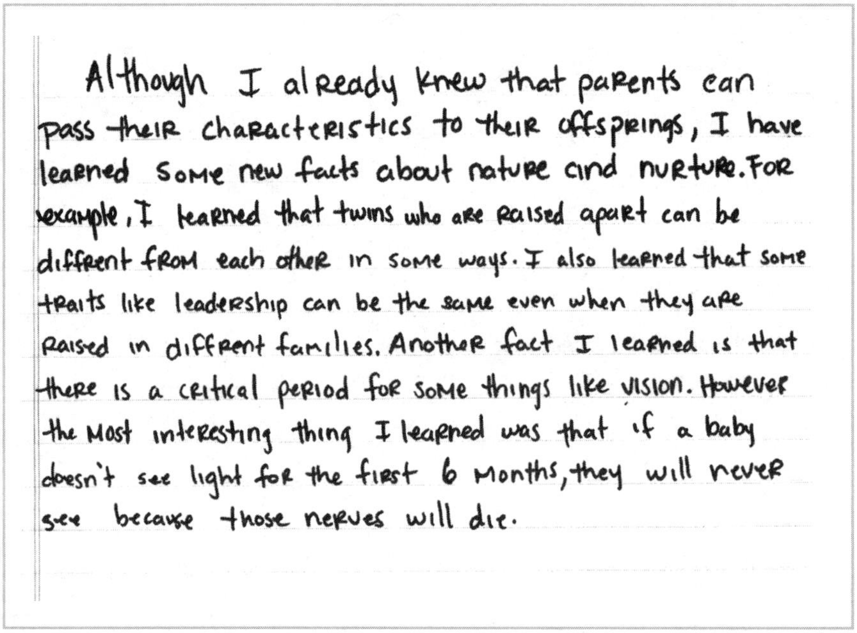

Although I already knew that parents can pass their characteristics to their offsprings, I have learned some new facts about nature and nurture. For example, I learned that twins who are raised apart can be different from each other in some ways. I also learned that some traits like leadership can be the same even when they are raised in different families. Another fact I learned is that there is a critical period for some things like vision. However the most interesting thing I learned was that if a baby doesn't see light for the first 6 months, they will never see because those nerves will die.

Figure 5.12 *Student writing using a frame*

this writing is increasingly academic (Jones and Thomas 2006). To accomplish this, students must consolidate their understanding of academic vocabulary. This individual task also allows teachers to determine their students' level of understanding of specific words and to make instructional decisions about which students need additional reteaching. See Figure 5.12 for a sample of student writing using the above writing frame.

■ Assessing Individual Learning of Academic Vocabulary

We've left the topic of assessment until now because we believe that measurement practices encompass the academic vocabulary learning across teacher modeling, peer interaction, and individual learning. At each point along the way, there should be formative assessment practices that parallel instructional goals. We agree with Blachowicz and Fisher's (2002) reminder that assessments should measure both the depth and the breadth of students' word knowledge. Therefore, multiple-choice quizzes that ask students to supply a single definition are unlikely to meet the depth criteria of good vocabulary assessment. In the same regard, artificially isolating words and testing them as if they were unrelated to other words and ideas won't get us to a measure of breadth. We know the lure of Scantron sheets can tempt us all into evaluating our students' vocabulary knowledge in this way. But just because it yields a number that we can write into a grade book doesn't mean we learned anything about what our students know.

Take a look at the assessment opportunities presented by the learning activities described in this book. To select an activity to use as an assessment, you first need to determine what you want to assess. Is it your students' existing knowledge? If so, a vocabulary self-awareness chart provides richer information than a multiple-choice test ever could. Do you want to look at vocabulary development over the course of a unit of study? Then an A–Z chart works well. To help you, we've listed dimensions of vocabulary assessment and corresponding activities from this book in Figure 5.13, p. 122.

■ Conclusion

The need for independent learning is critical by the time students reach adolescence, particularly because the adult world they will soon be entering demands independence. However, what passes for independent learning in many secondary classrooms has little to do with fostering independence. A necessary outcome of independent learning should be that learners grow as self-motivators, self-managers, and self-appraisers. As well, the needs of adolescents must be considered, particularly when it comes to choice, differentiation, and relevance.

Students can develop their own metacognition through activities like vocabulary self-awareness, A–Z charts, and vocabulary journals. All of these encourage students to be word users and to notice their own learning evolving over time. Individual learners also benefit from the physical and mental manipulation of words, as it allows them to develop extensive knowledge maps. Techniques such as word sorts and word cards draw their attention to the relationships between and among words. Keyword and peg mnemonics equip students with distinct study skills that help them master large amounts of information. In addition, composition activities like generative sentences and paragraph frames let learners experiment with words in context. Writing activities like this are not used at the beginning of word instruction; rather, they come after the learner has had opportunities to develop breadth and depth of vocabulary knowledge.

Dimension of Vocabulary Learning	Vocabulary Activity
Existing word knowledge	vocabulary self-awareness chart text impressions
Growth in vocabulary knowledge	A–Z chart vocabulary self-awareness chart
Application of vocabulary knowledge	generative sentences paragraph frames journals student think-alouds peer discussions
Word relationships (hierarchical and linear)	semantic feature analyses word maps shades of meaning word sorts
Knowledge of attributes	concept circles word maps word cards word sorts
Metacognitive awareness	vocabulary self-awareness chart student think-alouds mnemonics word cards word sorts

Figure 5.13 *Turning vocabulary learning into vocabulary assessment*

Make It a Priority
Creating a Schoolwide Focus on Learning Words

6

Miguel stopped Nancy in the hallway of Harrison Middle School to ask about corruption in Major League Baseball. He wanted to know more about the baseball owners' attempts to restrict players' salaries in the mid-1980s. Having had a class with her, Miguel knew that Nancy was not only interested in baseball but knew all kinds of sports trivia. Miguel was shocked to hear about secret deals between owners to limit how much they had to pay the major league players. Nancy knew that Miguel followed baseball, but she hadn't known he was curious about the sport's history. She wondered what had sparked this new interest. "The word *collusion* is one of this week's words," Miguel explained, "and Coach Williams used this baseball scandal as an example of that word in his class," Miguel said.

Vocabulary building in PE class . . . it doesn't get any better than this, Nancy thought to herself, smiling proudly.

To use the language of baseball, at Miguel's school, the entire faculty and student body team up to play ball with five words each week. *Collusion, cohere, collaborate, cooperate,* and *colleague* were selected to explore the Latin group of prefixes meaning closely or together. In this chance encounter in the hallway, Nancy furthered Miguel's understanding of one of the words. Then, pleased with Miguel's understanding of the word and this new interest, she dashed to the library later that day and with the help of the librarian found *Baseball and Billions: A Probing Look Inside the Business of Our National Pastime*, by Andrew Zimbalist (1994), and checked it out for Miguel. Miguel is a student who has to work hard to pass his classes, so Nancy wanted to do everything she could to keep his interest in baseball going.

Later that day, Nancy caught up with Miguel as he was heading down the hallway for the bus. "Hi, Miguel," Nancy said. "Look what I found in the library. If you want to read more about the scandal, this looks good."

"Sure," Miguel said with a slight smile. He tucked the book in his knapsack and ambled toward the bus.

This story sounds like one of those too-good-to-be-true scenes in a Hallmark Hall of Fame movie, but this kind of thing occurs often at Miguel's school—and in any school that sustains a schoolwide initiative. Efforts like words of the week and wide reading, during which students read books of their choice, often based on recommendations from teachers, extend students' thinking, vocabulary, and background knowledge. Look at what these two initiatives do for vocabulary learning in this school. They make word learning inescapable for kids, but in a way that has a sportlike, team-building spirit. Words get a workout all week; teachers make an effort to work them in to the day-to-day conversation, and in so doing, they send kids the message that vocabulary isn't the stuff of SAT prep, but the currency of talk, of socializing with peers, *and* of academic achievement.

As has been documented numerous times, schools with a clear focus outperform schools that lack a focus. For example, Reeves (2000) reported that establishing a schoolwide instructional focus was one of the most important actions that a school could take to improve performance. Similarly, in a study of middle and high schools that beat the odds, Langer (2001) reported that schoolwide attention to literacy was one of the indicators of successful performance. Given the importance of vocabulary, both for reading and writing, it seems reasonable to suggest academic vocabulary should become a schoolwide endeavor rather than be left up to the discretion of individual teachers. The two schoolwide efforts our research has shown to be effective are words of the week and wide reading.

■ Words of the Week

As we have noted throughout this book, students need to know a lot of words to be successful. They need to learn more than the words that are found in the current texts they're reading. We take exception with the idea that all of the words selected for instruction come from texts students are expect to read. While this view may be controversial in some circles, especially those who suggest that we teach words only in context, our experience indicates that sometimes students need to learn words that they will be able to use to figure out other words while reading. Of course, most of the words we teach are taught in context. Our out-of-context vocabulary work is known as the words of the week, or WOW, initiative.

The words of the week have a common prefix, suffix, root, or base. The primary goal is to provide students instruction in using these word parts to make educated guesses about unfamiliar words as they are reading. Engaging in a schoolwide focus on words of the week gives teachers an opportunity to provide vocabulary instruction relevant to their content area. All students learn the words, talk about the words, and are expected to add the words to their oral language and written vocabularies.

Arian is a student at our school. She immigrated from Pakistan with her mother and brother after her father was killed. She knew some English when she arrived. Consider Arian's increased knowledge about words following a week focused on five words containing the prefix *mal-*, meaning bad. The five example words were *malaria*, *malcontent*, *malodorous*, *malevolent*, and *malicious*. Even if Arian didn't master all five of these words, she would be likely to remember that *mal-* is bad and make an educated guess about meaning when she came into contact with words like *malformation* and *maladjusted*.

There is evidence that focusing on affixes and bases is helpful for students. For example, Baumann, Font, Edwards, and Boland (2005) examined the effectiveness of teaching word-part and context clues to promote word knowledge. According to their data, students must learn to use strategies and skills such as solving unknown words by understanding how affixes affect the meaning of root words. In their discussion about the myths and realities of teaching reading, Adams and Henry (1997) noted that attention to affixes was critical, especially after students had mastered early phonics. Without an increasingly sophisticated understanding of the ways words work, students fail to advance in their literacy skills.

If you doubt this at all, ask an informed and financially secure parent if he paid for an SAT prep course for his child. In that course, the student likely received more instruction on affixes than she received in all of her years in school combined. Understanding affixes and roots and bases helps us think about words. Yes, many teenagers forget what they learned in the SAT crash course. But imagine if this information were part of the regular school day, year after year. We just don't think that parents should have to pay for this instruction when we could infuse it into the school day.

The best implementation of WOW comes when the entire school agrees to focus on a small group of related words every week. Of course, an individual teacher can also implement a WOW initiative. When the entire school participates, the word lists can be generated well in advance of the school year. In some schools, a WOW committee identifies specific prefixes, suffixes, roots, and bases and sends this list to all teachers. Teachers then nominate words for inclusion on the list. The committee can then select the best examples for use during the school year. An example of one school's effort can be found in Figure 6.1.

The responsibility for teaching WOW words is divided among the departments. The English department introduces the words each week to students through direct instruction using word cards and word walls. Since all students take English, this ensures that everyone receives an initial exposure to the

Week 1	Week 2	Week 3	Week 4
suffix: -ness (state or condition)	prefix: mal- (bad)	prefix: ob- (against)	suffix: -able (able to)
haplessness	malevolent	obstinate	capable
wildness	malignant	obsequious	despicable
lowliness	maladjust	obtuse	implacable
bitterness	malady	obstreperous	variable
selflessness	malicious	oblique	enviable

Week 5	Week 6	Week 7	Week 8
root: fac, fic (make)	root: sur (above)	root: cog, gno (know)	prefix: sub (under)
benefactor	insurmountable	recognize	subjugate
refectory	surfeit	cognition	substrate
facsimile	resurgent	diagnosis	sublime
malefactor	insurrection	ignorant	suborn
fictive	surpass	incognito	subservient

Figure 6.1 *Sample WOW affixes, root, and word choices*

words. The other departments are responsible for utilizing the words according to their relation to content. For instance, the physical education teachers used *malodorous* to describe the condition of the locker rooms, while the biology and world history teachers made connections to *malaria*. The U.S. history teachers discussed the *malevolence* of Hitler and Mussolini, and the mathematics teachers joked about *malcontents* in their classrooms. The overall effect is that students are drenched in a rich stew of vocabulary that has derivational consistency.

Given that English teachers formally introduce the words, they need instructional strategies that initiate students to definitional meaning and encourage multiple exposures. One of the ways to increase attention to these words is to print them on card stock for each participating teacher so that each teacher can create a word wall. Some teachers add each of the five words each week to their word wall and create a semester-long list, while others have a set of five words up only for the given week. Of course, word walls aren't limited to high-frequency prefix, suffix, and root words. Many of the content teachers with whom we work include content words on their word walls.

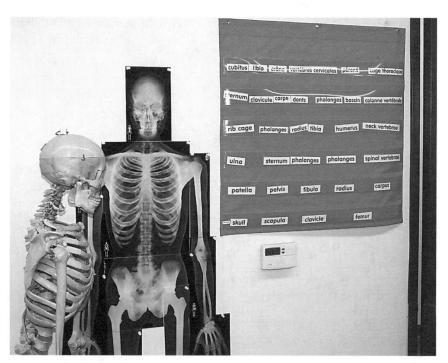

A word wall in biology

Using Word Walls in Content Area Classrooms

Word walls are an organized collection of words displayed in large letters on a wall. Simple enough. But students don't learn words from word walls by osmosis; simply being in the presence of words does not help students learn them. To be effective, words walls must be used. For example, teachers can review meanings of the word wall words, talking with students about definitions, additional examples, and related words. Students can write creative and interesting sentences using their word wall words. Of course, they should be asked to write sentences only after they have some familiarity with the words. Word walls help students remember words because of the frequency with which they can interact with the words. Most importantly, word wall interactions should be fun. Students can guess words based on information that the teacher provides. Alternatively, students can create bingo cards with the words and the teacher can call definitions until someone gets a bingo. We ask students to create vocabulary word cards for each of the words on the wall.

Figure 6.2 is a copy of a student-developed vocabulary card, based on the Frayer model discussed in Chapter 5 (Frayer, Frederick, and Klausmeier 1969). This particular card contains the word in the upper left quadrant, what the word means in the student's own words in the upper right quadrant, what the word doesn't mean or an antonym in the lower right quadrant, and an illus-

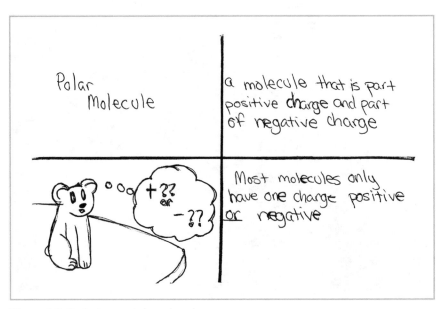

Figure 6.2 *Student-generated word card*

tration of the word in the lower left quadrant. Typically, these cards are hole-punched and maintained on a ring. We ask students to have five adults (family, coworkers, teachers, etc.) sign the back of each card following a conversation about what the word means. Not only does this increase the number of times the student interacts with the card, but it also provides students an authentic opportunity to use the word while speaking.

Over time, and with practice, students begin to incorporate words of the week into their oral and written vocabularies. For example, Ruben expressed his concern about school lunch with the comment, "Beyond unappealing, this sandwich is a prime example of the atrophy of our lunches." Another student was quoted as reporting "the belligerent behavior of a peer." Photography teacher Tricia Erickson from Northview High School in Grand Rapids, Michigan, has her students take photos and create images for the words they learn each week (see Figure 6.3 for a sample photo). It's her contribution to the overall vocabulary knowledge of students and she knows that she is doing her part to ensure that students learn words, inside and out.

Figure 6.3 *Student photography project illustrating weekly word*

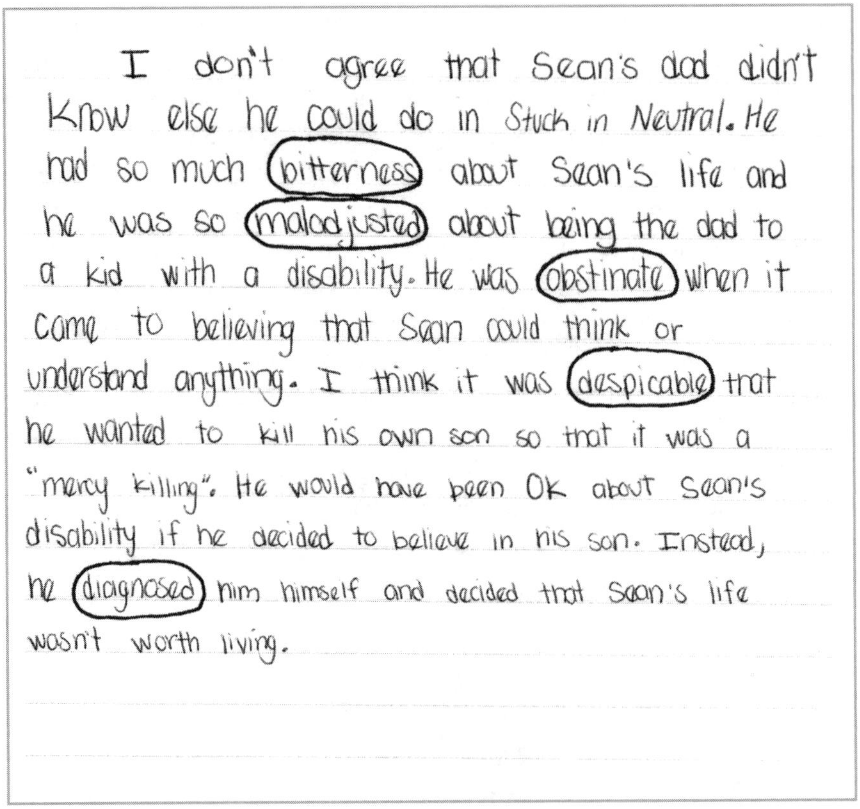

> I don't agree that Sean's dad didn't Know else he could do in *Stuck in Neutral*. He had so much (bitterness) about Sean's life and he was so (maladjusted) about being the dad to a kid with a disability. He was (obstinate) when it came to believing that Sean could think or understand anything. I think it was (despicable) that he wanted to kill his own son so that it was a "mercy killing". He would have been OK about Sean's disability if he decided to believe in his son. Instead, he (diagnosed) him himself and decided that Sean's life wasn't worth living.

Figure 6.4 *Writing sample containing words of the week*

Words of the week also appear in student's writing. Figure 6.4 contains a few paragraphs from Arian's writing. We've circled the words that were previously taught as part of the WOW program.

■ Building Word Knowledge Through Wide Reading

Amparo sits in her life sciences class, taking notes as Mr. Emerson introduces the genetics unit. At the mention of Gregor Mendel, her ears perk up. During the lab, Amparo calls Mr. Emerson over and says, "I actually know about this guy Mendel." Mr. Emerson gives her the look he's famous for—raising his bushy eyebrows and implying *Tell me more*. Amparo continues, "I was in the waiting room at the doctor's office last summer and read an article about him in a magazine." Mr. Emerson asks her what she recalls, and she reports, "He was a botanist, and he was a monk, too. He wrote about his experiments with

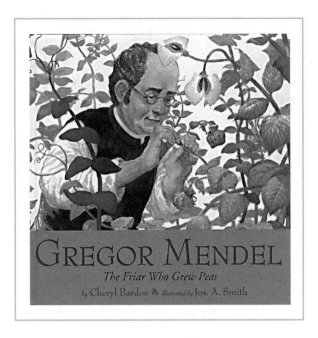

pea plants, but he was totally ignored until after he died. The writer told about another scientist who read [Mendel's] work and then wrote about it wrong, like on purpose, because he was jealous of Mendel."

Mr. Emerson, suitably impressed, offers Amparo a copy of *Gregor Mendel: The Friar Who Grew Peas* (Bardoe 2006) and says, "I just got this picture book on Mendel. If you're interested, I'd like to ask you to read it and let me know what you think of it."

How often have you met an articulate person and thought, *That's someone who's well read*? Amparo certainly fits that definition. The product of a person's reading habits are evidenced in her communications. It comes as no surprise to teachers that students who read more also possess a richer oral and written vocabulary (Stanovich and Cunningham 1992). Repeated exposure to the printed word results in a growing mental vocabulary bank in much the same way that exercise improves muscle memory.

The Cumulative Effects of Lots of Reading Experiences

Contact with print has a cumulative effect as the reader encounters known and unknown words. Consider the findings regarding the average number of words learned over the course of a school year, which far exceed the amount taught through direct instruction. By some estimates, students working at grade level learn about 3,000 new words per year (White, Graves, and Slater 1990), although only 300 to 500 can be reasonably taught directly (Mason et al. 2003). These same authors applied a simple algorithm to project the number of new words a well-read student (defined as one who reads sixty minutes per day, five days a week) would learn over the course of a year. That theoretical learner would encounter 2,250,000 words per year, of which approximately 2 to 5 percent would be unfamiliar to the reader. (This figure is derived from accepted understandings of what constitutes an independent level of reading.) Given that readers permanently acquire knowledge of 5 to 10 percent of those unknown words (Nagy and Herman 1987), Mason et al. (2003) estimated that this student would learn at least 2,250 new words per year. Adams noted:

> While affirming the value of classroom instruction in vocabulary, we must also recognize its limitations. By our best estimates, the growth in recognition vocabulary of the school age child typically exceeds 3,000 words per year, or more than eight per day. This order of growth cannot be ascribed to their classroom instruction, nor could it be attained through any feasible program of classroom instruction. (1990, 172)

Of course, teachers also know that you can't count on students reading for an hour a day, every day. Although this habit is vital for building background knowledge and vocabulary knowledge (Marzano 2004), students come to our classrooms exhibiting a disparate range of exposure to print. A widely cited study of the reading habits of fifth graders outside the school day found that this range varied from zero to ninety minutes per day, when all text was accounted for (Anderson, Wilson, and Fielding 1988). On average, these students read for thirteen minutes daily, or just over six hundred thousand words per year. Many schools have responded to this unequal distribution of reading experiences by fostering wide reading through sustained silent reading (SSR) and independent reading programs. Schoolwide wide reading and successful SSR and independent reading programs become additional tools for fostering academic vocabulary development in secondary schools.

Considering Wide Reading

Wide reading serves as a useful umbrella term for a host of reading programs and approaches that seek to foster reading habits among students. Learners who read widely, that is, from a broad range of texts, read for a variety of purposes. They seek information, entertainment, and diversion from print and digital sources. This includes books, of course, but also newspapers, comic books, websites, graphic novels, pamphlets, and virtually any other print matter you can imagine.

Wide reading has most commonly been associated with education in Great Britain, Australia, and New Zealand, where secondary students participate in wide reading courses designed to encourage a richer reading diet by extending their exposure to genres and texts. Some of these programs focus exclusively on canonical literature (the classics), but many now seek to interest and motivate adolescents through practices that allow learners to develop a growing sense of self-awareness as readers. In the United States, wide reading refers to the in- and out-of-school practices of learners who engage with a variety of genres. In-school approaches to wide reading include sustained silent reading, which allows for student choice in what is read, and independent reading, where students are given blocks of uninterrupted time to read content-aligned material.

Learning Vocabulary from Wide Reading

The debate for many years on vocabulary development was whether one learned more effectively from definitional instruction or from context. One camp posited that learning formal definitions was the best way, while others claimed that you needed to learn contextually, that is, through instruction that highlighted the use of a term with a sentence or paragraph. Let's take the word *botanist*, which Amparo used in her recount of the article about Mendel. Those who favored definitional instruction would assert that the best way for Amparo to understand this word would be to learn that it is a noun and that it describes a person with formal scientific training in plants. They would favor instruction that included its use in a sentence: *The botanist used his knowledge of plants to diagnose Dutch elm disease*. Others would argue that Amparo would best learn this word through context—through the reading of a longer piece of text that utilized this term. As you can probably guess, we think that both are critical to improving students' academic vocabulary knowledge.

Although Amparo's acquisition of *botanist* may have been incidental, there were factors working in her favor. A meta-analysis of twenty studies on vocabulary learning during reading found that students in upper grade levels, those who read more proficiently, and those who possessed some partial word knowledge of unfamiliar terms were likely to successfully learn up to 15 percent of those new words, if the text wasn't exceedingly difficult (Swanborn

Student engaged in independent reading

and deKlopper 1999). Those are a lot of qualifications, but they serve as a bell-wether for educators who are establishing wide reading programs to support vocabulary development:

- In order for students to benefit, the text needs to be instructionally useful and not too difficult.

- Older readers overall make larger strides than young children, most likely because they can call upon a larger cache of strategies for approaching unfamiliar words.

- The new words they are most likely to learn are the ones that they know a little bit about.

- The stronger readers are going to make larger gains in vocabulary acquisition than the less proficient (Swanborn and deKlopper 1999).

INCIDENTAL VOCABULARY LEARNING

As noted earlier, wide reading is of educational interest in part because of the connection to incidental vocabulary learning. Learning becomes incidental when it occurs as an unplanned (although not necessarily unintentional) event. Consider your own incidental learning that might occur as you watched someone complete a task like preparing a turkey for a Thanksgiving dinner. In all likelihood, you would not only learn how to prepare and baste the turkey but also pick up a few other hints along the way, such as the best technique for lifting it out of the roasting pan without dropping it or burning yourself. Incidental learning is a vital part of the learning design of simulations because marshaling complex tasks can't be effectively taught in a strictly linear fashion. At some point, one has to consolidate a variety of skills into a seamless effort. Reading, for instance, occurs in this way. At some point, the reader brings together her knowledge of symbols, sounds, syntax, semantics, and pragmatics and applies this knowledge to new texts.

At the same time, that same reader is growing her knowledge of reading by picking up helpful insights along the way. Stanovich (1986) has a term for this: the *Matthew effects* of reading, after the passage in the Bible's book of Matthew about the rich getting richer. Learners who read more get better at reading because of the incidental learning that occurs, and therefore, they read even more.

Stanovich's findings capture another essential factor in incidental learning: motivation. It appears that occurrences of incidental learning rise as motivation and interest increase. The turkey example is illustrative—your ability to notice details, pick up tips for success, and learn from someone else's mistakes increases if you are intrinsically interested in food preparation, or if you know that you will soon need to be able to do this yourself. Incidental learning of vocabulary occurs in much the same way. Readers who are interested in the topic at hand are likely to pick up more vocabulary along the way. Most of us have witnessed this in a young child with a deep interest in dinosaurs, let's say. We marvel in his ability to spout off terms like *oviraptor* and *allosaurus* and correctly identify them in an illustration. In this case, the child's interest in the topic contributed to his incidental learning of this technical vocabulary.

Adolescents are no different; like all humans, their incidental learning increases when they are motivated and interested. In particular, their motivation is directed by their own goals for completing the reading (Guthrie and Wigfield 2000). These goals might include learning how to do something, being entertained, or acquiring more information about a topic of interest. As teachers, this can be a challenge at times. Topics of interest to our middle and high school students may not resonate with us. Therefore, knowing something about their interests is an important first step in acquiring reading materials for them to use.

Approaches to Wide Reading

Exposure to lots of reading material is an important component in a program to develop academic vocabulary, especially because of its contributions to building background knowledge (Marzano 2004) and incidental vocabulary learning (Swanborn and deKlopper 1999). Sustained silent reading and independent reading both provide students opportunities to extend their academic vocabulary knowledge.

SUSTAINED SILENT READING: GETTING HOOKED ON THE READING HABIT

Sustained silent reading is dedicated time set aside for students to read what they choose. It is designed to build reading habits, background knowledge, and vocabulary. As such, there is evidence that SSR contributes to students' positive attitudes toward reading (Yoon 2002). In addition, SSR has been found to be a contributory factor in positive achievements in school reform (Fisher 2004; Mosenthal et al. 2004). A comparative study of seventh- and eighth-grade students found that those who participated in an SSR program showed larger gains in vocabulary than those who received regular reading instruction (Holt and O'Tuel 1989).

We can't proceed in the conversation about SSR without addressing the National Reading Panel (2000) report. The urban legend surrounding this report is that the NRP said that in-school free reading programs don't work. However, that is a misinterpretation of the panel's report on fluency instruction, which states that while it was unable to draw a recommendation from the 14 studies it examined (from a pool of 603), it did recommend that further research be conducted (NRP 2000). What remains in evidence is a large body of research that the NRP was unable to consider because of its restrictive statistical methodology requirements. The report did not recommend, however, the suspension of wide reading at school.

An effective SSR program

The work of Janice Pilgreen (2000) has been instrumental in the success of secondary SSR programs across the country. She performed a meta-analysis of several studies on SSR to determine which factors contributed to a successful program and then implemented a series of studies with high school students. She found that there was a modest increase in reading achievement with SSR, as well as a statistically significant effect on interest and motivation toward reading. Following are the eight factors she identified:

- *Access*: Students need to be flooded with reading materials.

- *Appeal*: The reading materials should be geared toward the interests of the students who are reading them.

- *Conducive Environment*: The physical setting should be quiet and comfortable.

- *Encouragement*: Students need supportive adult role models who can offer assistance in locating reading material.

- *Staff Training*: SSR doesn't just happen; the staff of a school should be well versed in the goals and procedures used at the school.

- *Nonaccountability*: This is perhaps the most controversial factor. Pilgreen found that students read more, and had more positive attitudes toward reading, when book reports and such were not required.

- *Follow-Up Activities*: Pilgreen found that follow-up activities such as conversations about books read by students or the teacher encouraged others to try them out.

- *Distributed Time to Read*: A common error made by schools new to SSR is that they have one long SSR period a week, rather than shorter periods that occur daily. Pilgreen found that successful programs have students read for fifteen to twenty minutes daily.

These eight factors have been replicated in a study by Fisher (2004) on a high school SSR program. In addition, Marzano (2004) also found these factors to be necessary in order to develop a wide reading habit necessary for building background knowledge, and further found that these efforts need to be sustained for a year or more in order to reap the benefits.

Now let's look inside a classroom to see how SSR can be implemented. As the bell rings signaling the beginning of third period, Peter quickens his pace to enter the gym before Coach Velasquez closes the door. "Let's go, folks! SSR is starting. You know what to do." They do know what to do, since SSR at this school takes place at the same time each day, as its own period. For twenty minutes, students, teachers, administrators, and noninstructional personnel settle in with a good book (or a host of other reading materials). Some students walk to the back of the gym to choose a book from the coach's collection of SSR materials. There are quite a few items reflecting his interest in athletics, but there are also magazines, newspapers, and even a few driver education manuals from the state department of motor vehicles. Because nearly three hundred students take physical education during this period, the PE instructors keep reading materials that can be read in one sitting, including collections of short stories and titles from the Chicken Soup for the Soul series. Some students bring their own reading materials. For example, Amparo has brought her copy of the graphic novel *The Tale of One Bad Rat* (Talbot 1997), a story of abuse that was recommended by another student in the peer counseling program she joined last year.

Peter picks up a copy of *The Hammer* (Stone and Mravic 2007), a collection of articles published in *Sports Illustrated* between 1957 and 1994 on baseball legend Hank Aaron. He first thumbs through the glossy photographs of the African American outfielder who broke Babe Ruth's home run record in 1974. He chooses the article "End of the Glorious Ordeal," by Ron Fimrite (2007), because he figures that the ordeal referred to in the title is the race to the record. As he reads the following passage, he uses his problem-solving strategies to figure out some of the vocabulary:

> Downing's [the pitcher] momentous mistake was a high fastball into Aaron's considerable strike zone. Aaron's whip of a bat lashed out at it and snapped it in a high arc toward the 385-foot sign in left centerfield. (66)

Peter uses his background knowledge on baseball to understand terms like *fastball* and *strike zone*, and *arc* isn't a problem, either, because he's been using that word in geometry. However, two words cause him to stumble. *Considerable* is in relation to *strike zone*. He's familiar with *considerate* and knows that it means to be polite, to pay attention to someone. Maybe there's a link there, he thinks. It might be something worth paying attention to, like a big strike zone. He knows enough about baseball to understand that great batters can hit the ball from nearly anywhere and are tougher to pitch to because you can't get one past them. He rereads, substituting the word *large*, and is satisfied with

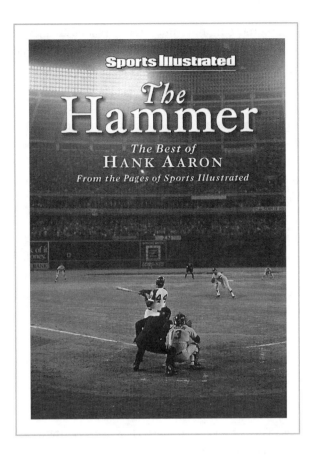

the meaning. The other problem is *whip of a bat*. Knowing the words isn't the trouble; it's the syntax. When he reads *whip* the first time, he thinks of a noun. But the meaning of the sentence breaks down when he realizes that doesn't work. He rereads and discovers that it's a noun phrase (although he doesn't consciously label it this way) and that the writer is using *whip* as a metaphor to illustrate how quick Aaron's swing is.

Peter continues to read until the bell signaling the end of SSR sounds twenty minutes later. As he trundles down off the bleachers with the other students, he passes his PE teacher. "Good book, Coach," he comments as he returns it to the rolling library cart where the books are stored. "You should read it."

INDEPENDENT READING: APPLYING WHAT IS KNOWN IN CONTENT TEXTS

Independent reading differs from sustained silent reading in one key regard: the amount of choice. Students participating in SSR select texts from a host of materials, including those that are not directly related to a content area. Students engaged in independent reading choose reading materials from those selected by the teacher based on the content or topic under investigation.

The ability to be able to read longer texts in order to support one's learning becomes critical at the secondary level. As subject matter becomes more complex, it becomes necessary to assign reading in order for learners to acquire a broader and deeper knowledge of the topic. The amount of assigned reading rises rapidly in postsecondary schooling, and college students are expected to read outside of class. Most of us recall the daunting reading lists we received with our syllabi in our undergraduate courses.

In middle and high school, the amount of time allotted to independent reading of content material varies widely. It is most common as a daily practice in English and history classes and may occur less frequently in mathematics and elective courses. For some teachers, independent reading is connected to a research project. In any case, the conditions for learning described in earlier chapters apply to independent reading. They include

- *Choice*: Students' ability to exercise some choice in what they read contributes to adolescent learning.

- *Relevance*: The texts identified must be perceived as useful to the learner, often through completion of a task.

- *Differentiation*: The average secondary classroom is attended by a range of students who read anywhere from several years below grade level to post–high school level. The range of readability of assigned materials should coincide with the range of learners. And remember, students do not acquire vocabulary from texts that are too difficult (Swanborn and deKlopper 1999).

Some teachers may need to broaden their definition of what constitutes content reading material. We include picture books, compilations of previously published articles, photo-essays, newspapers and magazines, and Web-based readings. By using richly detailed source materials such as these, we are able to meet the conditions for learning. These reading materials are especially valuable in courses like history and science, where timely information is essential to supplement textbooks written and published years earlier. Let's look at how two teachers use independent reading in their courses.

Ms. Baker's life science students have been learning about the anatomy and physiology of plants and are gathering research for an essay they will write on

Reading from a collection of books in geography

an aspect of a plant's structure and function. Students have signed up to research flowering plants, trees, and aquatic vegetation. Two students, Tiffany and DeJuan, are researching different aspects of tree life. Ms. Baker has amassed an extensive collection of books (see Figure 6.5 for a sample of books related to trees) and Tiffany and DeJuan have each selected a text. Since Tiffany's assigned topic is on the structure and function of tree levels, she first checks the table of contents for guidance. The book she has chosen, *Trees* (Julivert 2006), lists a section called "The Leaves: Nutrition for Trees." A proficient reader, she scans the pages quickly in order to locate the information she needs for her paper. "Top and Bottom," reads one section. *No*, she quickly decides, *I don't need to know much about the top and bottom of leaves.* "Photosynthesis" catches her eye, and she slows down to read more carefully. That's a term that has been used a lot in class, but she still doesn't really understand it. She reads:

> Using the water drawn through roots, the CO_2 taken in from the air, the sun's energy, and a molecule called chlorophyll (the green in leaves), which uses energy from the sun to synthesize carbohydrates from CO_2 and water (photosynthesis), leaves are able to produce sugars and other compounds and to release oxygen into the atmosphere. (10)

Arlon, P. 2006. *Tree: Discovery Starts with a Single Word*. New York: DK.

Blackaby, S. 2005. *The World's Largest Plants: A Book About Trees*. Mankato, MN: Picture Window Books.

Cassie, B. 1999. *Trees: National Audubon Society First Field Guide*. New York: Scholastic.

DK Publishing. 2005. *Tree: Eyewitness Books*. New York: Author.

Hibbert, C. 2004. *The Life of a Tree*. Portsmouth, NH: Raintree.

Julivert, M. A. 2006. *Trees: Field Guides*. New York: Enchanted Lion Books.

Figure 6.5 *Books about trees*

She recognizes the density of the text and knows that she needs to make sure she understands what she has read. She first consults a diagram nearby that illustrates the process, noting how the CO_2 enters the stoma of the leaves and O_2 exits. *Stoma* wasn't in the sentence she just read, so she consults the text again and this time notices the words *taken in* and *release*. Suddenly, it becomes clear to her—her understanding to this point had been at the process level, especially as it related to some of the chemistry involved. But she hadn't thought closely about the mechanics behind the process, especially just

how the gases entered and exited the leaves. By consolidating her knowledge of Tier 2 and Tier 3 vocabulary with the illustration, Tiffany has made an important leap in her understanding.

To her right, DeJuan is reading a different book from the selection. DeJuan reads two years below grade level, so this choice is a good fit for him. *Tree: Eyewitness Books* (DK Publishing 2005) augments written text with distinctive photographs full of detail, and DeJuan uses these as a guide to locate information. His report will be on coniferous trees, and in a short time he has located a section called "Chilly Trees." His eyes are drawn to the large print and accompanying illustrations labeled *leaves*, *cone*, and *seeds*, and he studies them for a few moments before searching out the written details. He reads,

> Conifers don't have flowers. Instead they have cones that hold seeds. When a cone falls it is often open and the seeds have dropped out. (13)

The short sentences allow him to digest the information in small chunks. He notices that *cone* and *conifer* begin with the same letters and realizes that the second term is derived from its distinctive feature. For both Tiffany and DeJuan, being able to choose from a range of texts allows them to deepen their understanding of the concepts they are learning. In both cases, the vocabulary of the classroom is being reinforced in the books they are reading. Ms. Baker's selection of these books was not accidental. She chose them for three reasons: the integrity of the information, the readability, and the use of content vocabulary to extend learning.

For English teachers, independent reading is a part of the daily flow of the class. Mr. Kim's class is reading *Season of Migration to the North* (Salih 2003), a novel translated from Arabic about a young man who returns to his native Sudan after attending college in England. The story is an exemplar of a universal theme—a stranger comes to town—and Mr. Kim reinforces this universality by providing a book list of titles with the same theme (see Figure 6.6 for a sample of the range of texts available on this theme). Students choose a title from the list, which offers a range of readability, and read and discuss the book with other members of the class reading the same book. Mr. Kim also looks for books that will appeal to the interests of these high school juniors and seniors, so some of the titles represent edgier topics, such as *The Devil and Miss Prym* (Coehlo 2002). Books are selected by the students, not assigned, but if a parent has an objection, Mr. Kim uses the book list to help the parent and student find a title that is mutually satisfactory. He is committed to the use of supplementary texts in his classroom as a way to address the unique learner profiles of his students. In addition, they have opportunities to apply the

Capote, T. 1968. *In Cold Blood: A True Account of a Multiple Murder and Its Consequences*. New York: Modern Library.

Coelho, P. 2002. *The Devil and Miss Prym*. New York: Harper Collins.

Inge, W. 1994. *Four Plays: Picnic*. New York: Grove.

Kay, T. 2003. *The Valley of Light*. New York: Atria.

Paterson, K. 1998. *Jip: His Story*. New York: Puffin.

Salih, T. 2003. *A Season of Migration to the North*. New York: Penguin.

Sheppard, M. C. 2003. *Seven for a Secret*. Toronto, ON: Groundwood.

Figure 6.6 *Books on the theme "When a Stranger Comes to Town"*

conceptually bound vocabulary he introduces with the core text in their own independent reading.

■ Conclusion

Schoolwide initiatives raise word consciousness among the faculty and students because they communicate the powerful message that words matter. One such program is words of the week, which focuses on a small group of semantically and structurally related words. The purpose has less to do with memorizing the exact definitions of these words, and more to do with highlighting the meaning pattern present in the group so that students can apply the pattern to unfamiliar words.

Another schoolwide vocabulary initiative is a commitment to wide reading. Wide reading is am important component in an academic vocabulary program, although it should be clear that it does not replace direct instruction through teacher modeling. Nor should it be used as a substitute for the learning activities that foster peer interactions to build knowledge or individual learning through meaningful work with words. However, wide reading through SSR and independent reading allows students to extend their vocabulary learning in texts that build background knowledge and challenge them to apply word knowledge to new forms of information. We advocate for wide reading to be integrated into a larger overall initiative of academic vocabulary development that occurs across all content areas. Reading is a fundamental element to subject matter learning, and reading texts that extend that learning is beneficial for all.

Make It Your Own

How to Keep Learning About Academic Vocabulary

7

By now, you're probably asking yourself, *How can I summarize and synthesize all of the information I've read in this book?* We know that the information we've shared in these pages can be a bit overwhelming. We don't know anyone (including ourselves) who does all of these things on a daily basis. That really would be overwhelming and would prevent students from doing anything else!

We do know teachers, however, who focus regularly on academic vocabulary. We see it in their classrooms and in the performance of their students. In this final chapter, we'd like to provide some concluding thoughts and some additional resources we have found helpful in improving our academic vocabulary instruction. Figure 7.1 provides an overview of the lessons we've learned about vocabulary instruction.

■ Lessons Learned

Having transformed from teachers who taught vocabulary through telling into teachers who purposefully integrate academic vocabulary instruction into our classrooms, we've learned some things along the way. First, and most importantly, word selection is critical. Knowing the types of words students use and what words they need to learn helps in the selection process. We've also learned that selecting words with colleagues who teach the same classes is helpful, although the targeted academic vocabulary in one classroom, even from period

Things to Avoid	Things to Do More
• Neglect vocabulary	• Understand the difference between general, specialized, and technical vocabulary
• Teach one definition of a word	• Purposefully select academic vocabulary words for instruction
• Require that students look up word meanings in a dictionary	• Model vocabulary solving, especially using context clues, word parts, and resources
• Assess words out of context, especially with single definitions for words	• Provide students opportunities for peer interaction with the expectation that they will *use* their developing academic vocabulary
	• Examine students' academic vocabulary work for reteaching opportunities
	• Ensure that students read widely on a daily basis

Figure 7.1 *What we've learned about effective vocabulary instruction*

to period, may have to differ based on student need. Middle and high school teachers must know their students well to make these determinations, and they need to have the chance to make these decisions.

Second, we've learned that many students don't have mental models for solving unknown words. As such, we are big believers in the role that teacher modeling plays in students' academic vocabulary development. That's not to say that we think students will learn individual words during teacher modeling, but rather that they will learn a procedure for addressing their own vocabulary questions.

Third, we know that students need lots of opportunities to build and consolidate their academic vocabulary. As such, we have to structure classrooms so that students are expected to use the words we teach, both specialized and technical. As we have discussed, peer interaction is critical for vocabulary learning. As teachers, we simply must structure peer conversations and activities if we want to improve student engagement and achievement.

Fourth, we have learned that while modeling and peer interactions are critical components for effective academic vocabulary development, they are not in and of themselves enough to radically change word learning. Students must

Teachers planning word-learning instruction

consolidate their vocabulary learning during independent activities. And teachers should use this student work as an assessment opportunity, checking for understanding to ensure that students are truly expanding their knowledge.

And finally, we have long understood the importance of wide reading. We all benefit, in countless ways, from wide reading. We gain information and are entertained. And, along the way, we learn new concepts and words. Providing students with a steady diet of reading materials of all sorts ensures that they extend their knowledge of academic vocabulary, even in the absence of the teacher. We have learned through our own wide reading that there are excellent resources for teaching vocabulary. In the section that follows, we'd like to share some of these with you.

■ Teacher Resources for Academic Vocabulary Development

The following is a list of books we consult on a regular basis. They're the books we go to for answers.

- *The Vocabulary Book: Learning and Instruction*, by Michael F. Graves (2006): This book presents a four-part plan for vocabulary instruction: rich and varied language experiences, teaching individual words, teaching word-learning strategies, and fostering word consciousness. We especially appreciate the way that Graves explains the importance of being word conscious.

● *Teaching Vocabulary in All Classrooms*, by Camille Blachowicz and Peter Fisher (2002): Based on their extensive review of research, Blachowicz and Fisher explain the teaching of vocabulary in a number of categories including learning vocabulary from context, integrating vocabulary and reading strategy instruction, learning vocabulary in literature-based reading instruction, learning vocabulary in the content areas, using dictionaries and other references, and assessing vocabulary knowledge. We are especially indebted to this book for its focus on wordplay in the classroom.

● *Building Background Knowledge for Academic Achievement*, by Robert Marzano (2004): In one of our favorite books, Marzano makes the case that teachers should focus on wide reading and subject-specific vocabulary. He not only notes the importance of background knowledge in ensuring students are successful in school but also provides classroom examples across elementary, middle, and high school classrooms.

● *Bringing Words to Life: Robust Vocabulary Instruction*, by Isabel L. Beck, Margaret G. McKeown, and Linda Kucan (2002): Simply said, no library would be complete without this book. This comprehensive resource makes a compelling case for word selection and instructional routines. While we take minor exceptions, based on our work in middle and high schools, we have learned a great deal from this excellent resource.

■ Classroom Materials for Creating Word Wise and Content Rich Schools

In addition to professional reading materials, we know that classrooms need to have resources for students to continue their academic vocabulary development. Following is a list of materials useful in middle and high school classrooms interested in academic vocabulary.

Of course, we can't imagine a classroom without a good dictionary. But perhaps even more important are the growing number of content-specific dictionaries. For example, *The American Heritage Science Dictionary* (Editors of the American Heritage Dictionaries 2005) and *A Dictionary of Science*, by John Daintith (2005), are good choices for science teachers. Mathematics teachers will probably prefer *The Penguin Dictionary of Mathematics* (Nelson 2003) whereas an art teacher might appreciate *The Yale Dictionary of Art and Artists* (Langmuir and Lynton 2000).

There are also a number of online dictionaries available on the Internet that teachers can bookmark. Our classroom computer bookmarks include

- *General Words*: www.m-w.com (Merriam-Webster)

- *Visual Dictionary*: www.infovisual.info

- *Rhyming Words (especially those with multiple syllables)*: www.rhymezone.com

- *Spanish Language*: www.spanishdict.com

- *World Languages*: www.wordreference.com

- *Thesaurus*: www.bartleby.com/thesauri

Using these dictionaries, you can develop favorite activities to do with your students. For example, you can teach students cutting-edge words by logging on to *Merriam-Webster's Collegiate Dictionary* (2005; www.m-w.com /info/new_words.htm) (Bromley 2007). Or you might have students use them to play the classic dictionary game, where players take turns finding an obscure word related to the content area, say just the word to the other players, and then players write convincing definitions on slips of paper. The player who found the word reads aloud the student-written definitions—along with a slip of paper containing the dictionary definition—and players vote on which one is the real definition. Whichever player garners the most votes wins the round. In addition to dictionaries, we strongly recommend the series of books related to vocabutoons. They are easy to use and students enjoy them. But more importantly, students learn from them. For more information about these books, visit www.vocabularycartoons.com.

Even well-read students are confounded at times by idioms, especially those that were popular in an earlier time. We keep a copy of *Webster's New World American Idioms Handbook* (Brenner 2003) available for students to use when they encounter phrases like *loose cannon* and *pardon my French*. Speaking of which, we also keep a copy of the *American Slang Dictionary* (Spears 2006) on our own desks. It contains some vulgar language, so we don't keep it in the general collection, but students know they can use it as a reference when needed. We find it handy, too, for deciphering the sometimes impenetrable speech of our students.

Idioms and slang are a good note for us to end on, because it reminds us that our language is continually shaped by its users. In the same regard, its users influence academic vocabulary instruction. The needs of learners should determine the best path for instruction, the best alchemy of approaches that foster their academic growth. Teachers who are committed to sharing their content expertise should adapt and improve on the strategies discussed in this book according to their needs.

We've spoken throughout this book about the notion of learning words inside and out. We've explored this phrase in a number of ways, but we'd like to summarize our thinking here. At the surface level, learning words inside and out refers to the need for deep meaning. As we learned from observing D'Andre, students need to know words well. They need to understand the nuances and connotations words have and learn to use precise vocabulary in their speaking and writing.

Second, we presented an approach to figuring out unknown words that also uses an inside and out approach. Readers can sometimes figure out words from looking outside of the word and other times from looking inside the word. Through teacher modeling and practice, students learn to use both inside and outside strategies for determining word meanings, especially for unknown words they encounter while reading.

And finally, we know that learning words inside and out can refer to the environments in which students use and learn academic vocabulary. When our teaching is at its best, our students take what they've learned inside our classrooms to their outside lives. Vocabulary doesn't exist between the school bells—it is carried with each learner for the rest of his or her life.

References

Chapter 1

BAKER, L. 1985. "Differences in the Standards Used by College Students to Evaluate Their Comprehension of Expository Text." *Reading Research Quarterly* 20: 297–313.

BAKER, S. K., D. C. SIMMONS, AND E. J. KAMEENUI. 1998. "Vocabulary Acquisition: Research Bases." In *What Reading Research Tells Us About Children with Diverse Learning Needs*, ed. D. C. Simmons and E. J. Kameenui, 183–218. Mahwah, NJ: Lawrence Erlbaum.

BECK, I. L., M. G. MCKEOWN, AND L. KUCAN. 2002. *Bring Words to Life: Robust Vocabulary Instruction*. New York: Guilford.

CRONBACH, L. J. 1942. "An Analysis of Techniques for Systematic Vocabulary Testing." *Journal of Educational Research* 36: 206–17.

DALE, E., J. O'ROURKE, AND H. A. BAMMAN. 1971. *Techniques for Teaching Vocabulary*. Palo Alto, CA: Field Educational.

EDWARDS, J. A., AND E. W. HAMILTON. 2006. *The Great American Mousical*. New York: HarperCollins.

FARLEY, M. J., AND P. B. ELMORE. 1992. "The Relationship of Reading Comprehension to Critical Thinking Skills, Cognitive Ability, and Vocabulary for a Sample of Underachieving College Freshmen." *Educational and Psychological Measurement* 52: 921–31.

FISHER, D. 2007. "Creating a Schoolwide Vocabulary Initiative in an Urban High School." *Journal of Education for Students Placed at Risk* 12 (3): 1–15.

FISHER, D., AND N. FREY. 2008. *Improving Adolescent Literacy: Content Area Strategies at Work*. 2d ed. Upper Saddle River, NJ: Merrill Prentice Hall.

FISHER, D., N. FREY, AND D. WILLIAMS. 2002. "Seven Literacy Strategies That Work." *Educational Leadership* 60 (3): 70–73.

FLOOD, J., D. LAPP, AND D. FISHER. 2003. "Reading Comprehension Instruction." In J. Flood, D. Lapp, J. R. Squire, and J. M. Jensen (eds.), *Handbook of Research on Teaching the English Language Arts*, Second Edition: 931–41. Mahwah, NJ: Lawrence Erlbaum Associates.

FRANCIS, M. A., AND M. L. SIMPSON. 2003. "Using Theory, Our Intuition, and a Research Study to Enhance Students' Vocabulary Knowledge." *Journal of Adolescent and Adult Literacy* 47: 66–78.

GRAVES, M. F. 1986. "Vocabulary Learning and Instruction." *Review of Educational Research* 13: 49–89.

———. 2006. *The Vocabulary Book: Learning and Instruction*. New York: Teachers College.

HATANO, G., AND K. IGNAKI. 1986. "Two Courses of Expertise." In *Child Development and Education in Japan*, ed. H. Stevenson, H. Azuma, and K. Hakuta, 262–72. New York: W. H. Freeman.

LASKY, K. 2002. *A Time for Courage: The Suffragette Diary of Kathleen Bowen, Washington, DC, 1917*. New York: Scholastic.

MCKEOWN, M. G. 1985. "The Acquisition of Word Meaning from Context by Children of High and Low Ability." *Reading Research Quarterly* 20: 482–95.

NAGY, W. E., AND R. C. ANDERSON. 1984. "How Many Words Are There in Printed School English?" *Reading Research Quarterly* 19: 303–30.

NATIONAL RESEARCH COUNCIL. 1999. *How People Learn: Brain, Mind, Experience, and School.* Ed. J. D. Bransford, A. L. Brown, and R. R. Cocking. Committee on Developments in Science of Learning. Washington, DC: National Academy Press.

PATCHETT, A. 2005. *Bel Canto.* New York: Harper Perennial.

SCARBOROUGH, H. S. 2001. "Connecting Early Language and Literacy to Later Reading (Dis)abilities: Evidence, Theory, and Practice." In *Handbook for Research in Early Literacy*, ed. S. Neuman and D. Dickinson, 97–110. New York: Guilford.

STEVENS, R. J. 2006. "Integrated Middle School Literacy Instruction." *Middle School Journal* 38 (1): 13–19.

VACCA, R. T., AND J. A. VACCA. 2007. *Content Area Reading: Literacy and Learning Across the Curriculum.* 9th ed. Boston: Allyn and Bacon.

■ Chapter 2

ALLEN, T. B. 2004. *George Washington, Spymaster: How the Americans Outspied the British and Won the Revolutionary War.* Washington, DC: National Geographic.

BECK, I. L., M. G. MCKEOWN, AND L. KUCAN. 2002. *Bring Words to Life: Robust Vocabulary Instruction.* New York: Guilford.

BORING, M. 2005. *Guinea Pig Scientists: Bold Self-Experimenters in Science and Medicine.* New York: Henry Holt.

COXHEAD, A. 2000. "A New Academic Word List." *TESOL Quarterly* 34 (2): 213–38.

FISHER, D. 2004. "Setting the 'Opportunity to Read' Standard: Resuscitating the SSR Program in an Urban High School." *Journal of Adolescent and Adult Literacy* 48: 138–50.

FISHER, D., J. FLOOD, D. LAPP, AND N. FREY. 2004. "Interactive Read-Alouds: Is There a Common Set of Implementation Practices?" *The Reading Teacher* 58: 8–17.

FISHER, D., AND N. FREY. 2008. *Improving Adolescent Literacy: Content Area Strategies at Work.* Upper Saddle River, NJ: Pearson Merrill Prentice Hall.

FISHER, D., C. ROTHENBERG, AND N. FREY. 2007. *Language Learners in the English Classroom.* Urbana, IL: National Council of Teachers of English.

FRAYER, D. A., W. C. FREDERICK, AND H. J. KLAUSMEIER. 1969. *A Schema for Testing the Level of Concept Mastery.* Working Paper No. 16. Madison: Wisconsin Research and Development Center for Cognitive Learning.

GRAVES, M. F. 2006. *The Vocabulary Book: Learning and Instruction.* New York: Teachers College.

MARZANO, R. J., AND D. J. PICKERING. 2005. *Building Academic Vocabulary: Teacher's Manual.* Alexandria, VA: Association for Supervision and Curriculum Development.

NAGY, W. E. 1988. *Teaching Vocabulary to Improve Reading Comprehension.* Urbana, IL: National Council of Teachers of English.

NAGY, W. E., AND P. A. HERMAN. 1987. "Breadth and Depth of Vocabulary Knowledge: Implications for Acquisition and Instruction." In *The Nature of Vocabulary Acquisition*, ed. M. G. McKeown and M. E. Curtis, 19–36. Hillsdale, NJ: Lawrence Erlbaum.

OGDEN, C. K. 1930. *Basic English: A General Introduction with Rules and Grammar.* London: Paul Treber.

PANCHYK, R. 2002. *World War II for Kids.* Chicago: Chicago Review.

PEARSON, P. D., AND G. GALLAGHER. 1983. "The Gradual Release of Responsibility Model of Instruction." *Contemporary Educational Psychology* 8: 112–23.

SCIENTIFIC PUBLISHING. 2007. *The Illustrated Atlas of Human Anatomy.* Elk Grove Village, IL: Author.

SCOTT, J. A., D. JAMIESON-NOEL, AND M. ASSELIN. 2003. "Understanding the Definitions of Unfamiliar Verbs." *Reading Research Quarterly* 32: 184–200.

SHRIVER, M. 2000. *Ten Things I Wish I'd Known—Before I Went Out into the Real World*. New York: Warner Books.

STAHL, S. A., AND M. M. FAIRBANKS. 1986. "The Effects of Vocabulary Instruction: A Model-Based Meta-analysis." *Review of Educational Research* 56 (1): 72–110.

WHITE, T. G., J. SOWELL, AND A. YANAGIHARA. 1989. "Teaching Elementary Students to Use Word-Part Clues." *The Reading Teacher* 42: 302–9.

▣ Chapter 3

ABBOTT, T. 2006. *Firegirl*. New York: Little, Brown.

AFFLERBACH, P., AND P. JOHNSTON. 1984. "On the Use of Verbal Reports in Reading Research." *Journal of Reading Behavior* 16: 307–22.

BECK, I. L., M. G. MCKEOWN, AND L. KUCAN. 2002. *Bringing Words to Life: Robust Vocabulary Instruction*. New York: Guilford.

BECK, I. L., M. G. MCKEOWN, AND E. S. MCCASLIN. 1983. "Vocabulary Development: All Contexts Are Not Created Equal." *The Elementary School Journal* 83: 177–81.

BEREITER, C., AND M. BIRD. 1985. "Use of Thinking Aloud in Identification and Teaching of Reading Comprehension Strategies." *Cognition and Instruction* 2: 131–56.

BROMLEY, K. 2007. "Nine Things Every Teacher Should Know About Words and Vocabulary Instruction." *Journal of Adolescent and Adult Literacy* 50: 528–37.

DAVEY, B. 1983. "Think Aloud: Modeling the Cognitive Processes of Reading Comprehension." *Journal of Reading* 27: 44–47.

DUFFY, G. G. 2003. *Explaining Reading: A Resource for Teaching Concepts, Skills, and Strategies*. New York: Guilford.

FARNDON, J. 2007. *Extreme Weather*. New York: Dorling Kindersley.

FARRIS, P. J., P. A. NELSON, AND S. L'ALLIER. 2007. "Using Literature Circles with English Language Learners at the Middle Level." *Middle School Journal* 38 (4): 38–42.

FISHER, D., AND N. FREY. 2008. *Better Learning Through Structured Teaching*. Alexandria, VA: Association for Supervision and Curriculum Development.

FISHER, D., N. FREY, AND D. LAPP. In press. "Shared Reading: Teaching Comprehension, Vocabulary, Text Structures, and Text Features." *The Reading Teacher*.

GEEK.COM. http://www.geek.com/convergence/

GORE, A. 2007. *An Inconvenient Truth: The Crisis of Global Warming (Adapted for a New Generation)*. New York: Penguin.

ISDELL, W. 1993. *A Gebra Named Al*. Minneapolis: Free Spirit.

JABLON, P. 2006. "Writing Through Inquiry." *Science Scope* 29 (7): 18–20.

LAPP, D., D. FISHER, AND M. GRANT. 2008. "'You Can Read This—I'll Show You How': Interactive Comprehension Instruction." *Journal of Adolescent and Adult Literacy* 51: 372–82.

WILFORD, S. 2007. "Modeling Appropriate Behaviors: Helping Teachers Recognize Their Position as Role Models for Children." *Early Childhood Today* 21 (5): 8–9.

WILHELM, J. 2001. *Improving Comprehension with Think-Aloud Strategies: Modeling What Good Readers Do*. New York: Scholastic.

▓ Chapter 4

ALVERMANN, D. E., AND P. R. BOOTHBY. 1982. *A Strategy for Making Content Reading Successful: Grades 4–6*. Paper presented at the annual meeting of the Plains Regional Conference of the International Reading Association, Omaha, NE, September.

ARONSON, J., N. BLANEY, C. STEPHIN, J. SIKES, AND M. SNAPP. 1978. *The Jigsaw Classroom*. Beverly Hills, CA: Sage.

BAUMANN, J. F., L. A. JONES, AND N. SEIFERT-KESSELL. 1993. "Using Think Alouds to Enhance Children's Comprehension Monitoring Abilities." *The Reading Teacher* 47: 184–93.

BECK, I. L., M. G. McKEOWN, AND L. KUCAN. 2002. *Bringing Words to Life: Robust Vocabulary Instruction*. New York: Guilford.

BURGER, S., AND M. CHRETIEN. 2001. "The Development of Oral Production in Content-Based Second Language Courses at the University of Ottawa." *Canadian Modern Language Review* 58 (1): 84–102.

BURKE, J. 2002. *Tools for Thought: Graphic Organizers for Your Classroom*. Portsmouth, NH: Heinemann.

CAZDEN, C. B. 2001. *Classroom Discourse: The Language of Teaching and Learning*. 2d ed. Portsmouth, NH: Heinemann.

DYKSTRA, P. 1994. "Say It, Don't Write It: Oral Structures as Framework for Teaching Writing." *Journal of Basic Writing* 13 (1): 41–49.

FARNDON, J. 2007. *Extreme Weather*. New York: Dorling Kindersley.

FISHER, A. L. 2001. "Implementing Graphic Organizer Notebooks: The Art and Science of Teaching Content." *The Reading Teacher* 55: 116–20.

FISHER, D., AND N. FREY. 2007. *Improving Adolescent Literacy: Content Area Strategies at Work*. 2d ed. Upper Saddle River, NJ: Pearson Merrill Prentice Hall.

GOODMAN, L. 2004. "Shades of Meaning: Relating and Expanding Word Knowledge." In *Teaching Vocabulary: 50 Creative Strategies, Grades K–12*, ed. G. E.

Tompkins and C. Blanchfield, 85–87. Upper Saddle River, NJ: Merrill Prentice Hall.

HATKOFF, I., C. HATKOFF, AND P. KAHUMBU. 2006. *Owen and Mzee: The True Story of a Remarkable Friendship*. New York: Scholastic.

HINTON, S. E. 1995. *The Outsiders*. New York: Penguin.

IVES, B. 2007. "Graphic Organizers Applied to Secondary Algebra Instruction for Students with Learning Disorders." *Learning Disabilities Research and Practice* 22: 110–18.

JACOBS, W. W. 1902. *The Monkey's Paw*. New York: Harper and Brothers.

JOHNSON, D. W., R. T. JOHNSON, AND K. SMITH. 1991. *Active Learning: Cooperation in the College Classroom*. Edina, MN: Interaction Book.

KAGAN, S. 1989. *Cooperative Learning Resources for Teachers*. San Juan Capistrano, CA: Resources for Teachers.

KOICHU, B., A. BERMAN, AND M. MOORE. 2007. "The Effect of Promoting Heuristic Literacy on the Mathematical Aptitude of Middle-School Students." *International Journal of Mathematical Education in Science and Technology* 38 (1): 1–17.

LYMAN, F. 1987. "Think-Pair-Share: An Expanding Teaching Technique." *MAA-CIE Cooperative News* 1: 1–2.

MCCAGG, E., AND D. DANSEREAU. 1991. "A Convergent Paradigm for Examining Knowledge Mapping as a Learning Strategy." *Journal of Educational Research* 84: 317–24.

MCGINLEY, W. J., AND P. R. DENNER. 1987. "Story Impressions. A Prereading/ Writing Activity." *Journal of Reading* 31: 248–54.

MORIN, R., AND J. GOEBEL JR. 2001. "Basic Vocabulary Instruction: Teaching Strategies or Teaching Words?" *Foreign Language Annals* 34 (1): 8–17.

MOUNTAIN, L. 2002. "Flip-a-Chip to Build Vocabulary." *Journal of Adolescent and Adult Literacy* 46: 62–68.

OCZKUS, L. D. 2003. *Reciprocal Teaching at Work: Strategies for Improving Reading Comprehension*. Newark, DE: International Reading Association.

OSTER, L. 2001. "Using the Think-Aloud for Reading Instruction." *The Reading Teacher* 55: 64–69.

PALINCSAR, A. S. 1987. "Reciprocal Teaching: Can Student Discussion Boost Comprehension?" *Instructor* 96 (5): 56–58, 60.

PITTELMAN, S. D., J. HEIMLICH, R. BERGLUND, M. FRENCH, AND J. E. HEIMLICH. 1991. *Semantic Feature Analysis: Classroom Application*. Newark, DE: International Reading Association.

RICHEK, M. A. 2005. "Words Are Wonderful: Interactive, Time-Efficient Strategies to Teach the Meaning of Words." *The Reading Teacher* 58: 414–25.

ROBINSON, D. H. 1998. "Graphic Organizers as Aids to Text Learning." *Reading Research and Instruction* 37: 85–105.

ROSENBAUM, C. 2001. "A Word Map for Middle School: A Tool for Effective Vocabulary Instruction." *Journal of Adolescent and Adult Literacy* 45: 44–49.

SELVIDGE, E. 2006. "Journey to Egypt: A Board Game." *Montessori Life: A Publication of the American Montessori Society* 18 (4): 36–39.

STAHL, S. A. 1999. *Vocabulary Development*. Newton Upper Falls, MA: Brookline.

WATSON, K. 1980. "A Close Look at Whole-Class Discussion." *English in Education* 14: 39–44.

WILHELM, J. D. 2001. "Think Alouds Boost Reading Comprehension." *Instructor* 111: 26–28.

YIP, F. W. M., AND A. C. M. KWAN. 2006. "Online Vocabulary Games as a Tool for Teaching and Learning English Vocabulary." *Educational Media International* 43: 233–49.

◼ Chapter 5

ALLEN, J. 2000. *Words, Words, Words: Teaching Vocabulary in Grades 4–12*. York, ME: Stenhouse.

BEAR, D. R., M. INVERNIZZI, S. R. TEMPLETON, AND F. JOHNSTON. 2007. *Words Their Way: Word Study for Phonics, Vocabulary, and Spelling Instruction*. 4th ed. Upper Saddle River, NJ: Prentice Hall.

BLACHOWICZ, C. L. Z., AND P. J. FISHER. 2002. *Teaching Vocabulary in All Classrooms*. 2d ed. Upper Saddle River, NJ: Merrill Prentice Hall.

FEARN, L., AND N. FARNAN. 2001. *Interactions: Teaching Writing and the Language Arts*. Boston: Allyn and Bacon.

FISHER, D., AND N. FREY. 2003. "Writing Instruction for Struggling Adolescent Writers: A Gradual Release Model." *Journal of Adolescent and Adult Literacy* 46: 396–407.

———. 2007. *Scaffolding Writing Instruction: A Gradual Release Model*. New York: Scholastic.

———. 2008. *Improving Adolescent Literacy: Content Area Strategies at Work*. 2d ed. Upper Saddle River, NJ: Merrill Prentice Hall.

FRAYER, D., W. C. FREDERICK, AND H. J. KLAUSMEIER. 1969. *A Schema for Testing the Level of Cognitive Mastery*. Madison, WI: Center for Education Research.

GOODWIN, L. 2001. "A Tool for Learning: Vocabulary Self-Awareness." In *Creative Vocabulary: Strategies for Teaching Vocabulary in Grades K–12*, ed. C. Blanchfield, 44–46. Fresno, CA: San Joaquin Valley Writing Project.

GRAFF, G., AND C. BIRKENSTEIN. 2006. *They Say / I Say: The Moves That Matter in Academic Writing*. New York: W. W. Norton.

JONES, R. C., AND T. G. THOMAS. 2006. "Leave No Discipline Behind." *The Reading Teacher* 60: 58–64.

LEWIS, M., AND D. WRAY. 1995. *Developing Children's Non-fiction Writing*. New York: Scholastic.

MURDOCH, K., AND J. WILSON. 2006. "Student Independent Learning." *Education Quarterly (Australia)*. Retrieved July 5, 2007, from www1.curriculum .edu.au/eq/summer2006/article1.html.

NAGY, W. E. 1988. *Teaching Vocabulary to Improve Reading Instruction*. Newark, DE: International Reading Association.

PAIVIO, A. 1969. "Mental Imagery in Associative Learning and Memory." *Psychological Review* 3: 241–63.

PIANTA, R. C., J. BELSKY, R. HOUTS, AND F. MORRISON. 2007. "Opportunities to Learn in America's Elementary Classrooms." *Science* 315: 1795–96.

PRESSLEY, M., J. R. LEVIN, AND H. D. DELANEY. 1983. "The Mnemonic Keyword Method." *Review of Educational Research* 52: 61–91.

RACE, P. 1996. "A Fresh Look at Independent Learning." Retrieved July 5, 2007, from www.city.londonmet.ac.uk/deliberations/eff.learning/indep.html.

RAUGH, M. R., AND R. C. ATKINSON. 1975. "A Mnemonic Method for Learning a Second-Language Vocabulary." *Journal of Educational Psychology* 67 (1): 1–16.

RIDLEY, D. S., P. A. SCHUTZ, R. S. GLANZ, AND C. E. WEINSTEIN. 1992. "Self-Regulated Learning: The Interactive Influence of Metacognitive Awareness and Goal-Setting." *Journal of Experimental Education* 60: 293–306.

RUDDELL, M. R., AND B. A. SHEARER. 2002. "'Extraordinary,' 'Tremendous,' 'Exhilarating,' 'Magnificent': Middle School At-Risk Students Become Avid Word Learners with the Vocabulary Self-Collection Strategy (VSS)." *Journal of Adolescent and Adult Literacy* 45: 352–63.

WEBER, B. 2004. *Animal Disguises*. Boston: Kingfisher.

■ Chapter 6

ADAMS, M. J. 1990. *Beginning to Read: Thinking and Learning About Print*. Cambridge, MA: MIT Press.

ADAMS, M. J., AND M. K. HENRY. 1997. "Myths and Realities About Words and Literacy." *School Psychology Review* 26: 425–36.

ANDERSON, R. C., P. T. WILSON, AND L. G. FIELDING. 1988. "Growth in Reading and How Children Spend Their Time Outside of School." *Reading Research Quarterly* 23: 285–303.

BARDOE, C. 2006. *Gregor Mendel: The Friar Who Grew Peas*. New York: Harry Abrams.

Baumann, J. F., G. Font, E. C. Edwards, and E. Boland. 2005. "Strategies for Teaching Middle-Grade Students to Use Word-Part and Context Clues to Expand Reading Vocabulary." In *Teaching and Learning Vocabulary: Bringing Research to Practice*, ed. E. H. Hiebert and M. L. Kamil, 179–205. Mahwah, NJ: Lawrence Erlbaum.

Fimrite, R. 2007. "End of the Glorious Ordeal." In *The Hammer: The Best of Hank Aaron from the Pages of Sports Illustrated,* ed. C. Stone and M. Mravic. Des Moines, IA: Sports Illustrated Books.

Fisher, D. 2004. "Setting the 'Opportunity to Read' Standard: Resuscitating the SSR Program in an Urban High School." *Journal of Adolescent and Adult Literacy* 48: 138–50.

Frayer, D., W. C. Frederick, and H. J. Klausmeier. 1969. *A Schema for Testing the Level of Cognitive Mastery*. Madison, WI: Wisconsin Center for Education Research.

Guthrie, J. T., and A. Wigfield. 2000. "Engagement and Motivation in Reading." In *Handbook of Reading Research*, ed. M. L. Kamil, P. B. Mosenthal, P. D. Pearson, and R. L. Barr, vol. III, 403–24. Mahwah, NJ: Lawrence Erlbaum.

Holt, S. B., and F. S. O'Tuel. 1989. "The Effect of Sustained Silent Reading and Writing on Achievement and Attitudes of Seventh and Eighth Grade Students Reading Two Years Below Grade Level." *Reading Improvement* 26: 290–97.

Langer, J. A. 2001. "Beating the Odds: Teaching Middle and High School Students to Read and Write Well." *American Educational Research Journal* 38: 837–80.

Marzano, R. J. 2004. *Building Background Knowledge for Academic Achievement: Research on What Works in Schools.* Alexandria, VA: Association for Supervision and Curriculum Development.

Mason, J. M., S. A. Stahl, K. H. Au, and P. A. Herman. 2003. "Reading: Children's Developing Knowledge of Words." In *Handbook of Research on Teaching the English Language Arts*, ed. J. Flood, D. Lapp, J. R. Squire, and J. M. Jensen, 2d ed., 914–30. Mahwah, NJ: Lawrence Erlbaum.

Mosenthal, J., M. Lipson, S. Torncello, B. Russ, and J. Mekkelsen. 2004. "Contexts and Practices of Six Schools Successful in Obtaining Reading Achievement." *Elementary School Journal* 104: 343–67.

Nagy, W. A., and P. A. Herman. 1987. "Breadth and Depth of Vocabulary Knowledge: Implications for Acquisition and Instruction." In *The Nature of Vocabulary Acquisition*, ed. M. G. McKeown and M. E. Curtis, 19–36. Hillsdale, NJ: Lawrence Erlbaum.

National Reading Panel (NRP). 2000. *Teaching Children to Read: An Evidence-Based Assessment of the Scientific Literature on Reading and Its Implications for Instruction: Report of the Subgroups.* Washington, DC: National Institute of Child Health and Human Development (NICHD).

PILGREEN, J. L. 2000. *The SSR Handbook: How to Organize and Manage a Sustained Silent Reading Program.* Portsmouth, NH: Boynton/Cook.

REEVES, D. 2000. *Accountability in Action: A Blueprint for Learning Organizations.* Denver: Advanced Learning Centers.

STANOVICH, K. E. 1986. "Matthew Effects in Reading: Some Consequences of Individual Differences in the Acquisition of Literacy." *Reading Research Quarterly* 21: 360–406.

STANOVICH, K. E., AND A. CUNNINGHAM. 1992. "Studying the Consequences of Literacy Within a Literate Society: The Cognitive Correlates of Print Exposure." *Memory and Language* 20: 51–88.

STONE, C., AND M. MRAVIC, EDS. 2007. *The Hammer: The Best of Hank Aaron from the Pages of Sports Illustrated.* Des Moines, IA: Sports Illustrated Books.

SWANBORN, M. S. L., AND K. DEKLOPPER. 1999. "Incidental Word Learning While Reading: A Meta-analysis." *Review of Educational Research* 69: 261–85.

TALBOT, B. 1997. *The Tale of One Bad Rat.* New York: Dark Horse.

WHITE, T. G., M. F. GRAVES, AND W. H. SLATER. 1990. "Growth of Reading Vocabulary in Diverse Elementary Schools: Decoding and Word Meaning." *Journal of Educational Psychology* 82: 281–90.

YOON, J. 2002. "Three Decades of Sustained Silent Reading: A Meta-analytic Review of the Effects of SSR on Attitude Toward Reading." *Reading Improvement* 39 (4): 186–95.

ZIMBALIST, A. 1994. *Baseball and Billions: A Probing Look Inside the Business of Our National Pastime.* New York: Basic Books.

Chapter 7

BECK, I. L., M. G. MCKEOWN, AND L. KUCAN. 2002. *Bringing Words to Life: Robust Vocabulary Instruction.* New York: Guilford.

BLACHOWICZ, C., AND P. FISHER. 2002. *Teaching Vocabulary in All Classrooms.* Upper Saddle River, NJ: Merrill Prentice Hall.

BRENNER, G. A. 2003. *Webster's New World American Idioms Handbook.* Indianapolis: Wiley.

BROMLEY, K. 2007. "Nine Things Every Teacher Should Know About Words and Vocabulary Instruction." *Journal of Adolescent and Adult Literacy* 50: 528–37.

EDITORS OF THE AMERICAN HERITAGE DICTIONARIES. 2005. *The American Heritage Science Dictionary.* Boston: Houghton Mifflin.

DAINTITH, J. 2005. *A Dictionary of Science.* 5th ed. New York: Oxford University Press.

GRAVES, M. F. 2006. *The Vocabulary Book: Learning and Instruction*. New York: Teachers College.

LANGMUIR, E., AND N. LYNTON. 2000. *The Yale Dictionary of Art and Artists*. New Haven, CT: Yale.

MARZANO, R. 2004. *Building Background Knowledge for Academic Achievement*. Alexandria, VA: Association for Supervision and Curriculum Development.

NELSON, D. 2003. *The Penguin Dictionary of Mathematics*. 3d ed. New York: Penguin.

SPEARS, R. A. 2006. *American Slang Dictionary*. 4th ed. New York: McGraw-Hill.

TALBOT, B. 1997. *The Tale of One Bad Rat*. Milwaukie, OR: Dark Horse.

Index